Rockets and Missiles
of Cape Canaveral

by Cliff Lethbridge

To Lee~
Thank you for
your favorable
comments on this book~
Hope you enjoy this
"full color" edition~
Thanks Again!
CJL

Rockets and Missiles of Cape Canaveral

By Cliff Lethbridge

Published by Spaceline, Inc.

Cape Canaveral, Florida

First Edition June, 2017

Graphic Design and Typesetting: Ryon Speir

Project Supervisor: Stacey Norman

Photo Selection: Al Hartmann

Photos Courtesy:

U.S. Air Force, U.S. Army, U.S. Navy, NASA, United Launch Alliance, SpaceX

Front Cover Center Photo:

Delta IV

Front Cover Surrounding Photos Clockwise From Top Left:

Mercury-Atlas, Delta II 7000 Series, Pershing II, Alpha Draco, Atlas V, Trident II, Juno II, Mercury-Redstone, Commercial Titan III, Atlas F, Space Shuttle Discovery, Jupiter

Back Cover Photo:

Falcon 9 Full Thrust

For more information regarding Cape Canaveral, visit www.spaceline.org

To contact the author, e-mail clifflethbridge@spaceline.org

Table of Contents

Cape Canaveral "Missile Row" looking north, 1964

BUMPER-WAC

Classification: Research Rocket

Length: 62 feet

Diameter: 5 feet, 5 inches

Finspan: 12 feet

Date of First Cape Canaveral Launch: July 24, 1950

Date of Final Cape Canaveral Launch: July 29, 1950

Number of Cape Canaveral Launches: 2

Although flown just twice from Cape Canaveral, the Bumper-Wac will always deserve a prominent place in history because of its location in the Cape's launch chronology.

Indeed, the last two Bumper-Wac missiles ever flown represented the first and second launches from Cape Canaveral's fledgling missile testing grounds.

A marriage of the German V-2 ballistic missile and the U.S. Army Wac Corporal research rocket, the Bumper-Wac design can be traced back to the creation of the Wac Corporal in 1944.

At that time, the Wac Corporal was designed and built in a cooperative effort between Douglas Aircraft and the Guggenheim Aeronautical Laboratory, in association with the Jet Propulsion Laboratory at California Institute of Technology.

The cooperative group designed and built a 5-foot long solid-fueled booster called "Tiny Tim" which could produce an impressive thrust of 50,000 pounds.

"Tiny Tim" was attached to the bottom section of a 20-foot liquid-fueled sustainer engine stage, with the total vehicle capable of reaching a speed of nearly 3,000 m.p.h. on ascent. This two-stage combination comprised the Wac Corporal research rocket.

The actual Bumper-Wac configuration was designed in support of "Project Hermes", an Army research effort conducted between 1948 and 1952.

A vehicle was needed to facilitate the study of technical problems associated with rocket stage separation, high altitude flight dynamics and high altitude rocket stage ignition.

A total of eight captured German V-2 ballistic missiles were adapted for the tests. The Wac Corporal's liquid-fueled stage was simply mounted on the nose of the V-2 to create the Bumper-Wac.

The Wac Corporal's "Tiny Tim" solid-fueled stage was not employed in the Bumper-Wac combination. The liquid-fueled stage alone, as adapted for the vehicle, was 15 feet long and 1 foot wide and could produce a thrust of 150 pounds.

The V-2 stage was 45 feet long and 5 feet, 5 inches wide with a total finspan of 12 feet. It could produce a thrust of 55,000 pounds at liftoff.

The Wac Corporal second stage remained atop the nose of the V-2 for the first minute of flight. The V-2 then shut down, after providing a high altitude "bump" for the Wac Corporal second stage. This is why the V-2 first stage was given the name "Bumper".

Following the first stage shutdown, the Wac Corporal second stage ignited and fired for 45 seconds, completing the remainder of the flight.

The first six Bumper-Wac rockets were launched from the White Sands Missile Range in New Mexico. The first of these was launched on May 13, 1948. The vehicle flew to an altitude of 80 miles at a maximum speed of 2,740 m.p.h.

Five more test flights were conducted at White Sands with mixed results. Bumper #5, launched on February 24, 1949 was the most successful in the White Sands Bumper-Wac series. In this test, the vehicle achieved an altitude of 244 miles at a maximum speed of 5,150 m.p.h. This marked the first time a man-made object reached space.

In 1950, Bumper-Wac tests moved to Cape Canaveral. Bumper #7 was scheduled to be launched first, but its initial launch attempt on July 19, 1950 was halted due to a failure of the first stage to achieve proper liftoff thrust.

The failure was traced to a stuck fuel valve which had become corroded by salt air and moisture. Thus, perhaps prophetically, the very first launch attempt from Cape Canaveral resulted in a "scrub".

The launch of Bumper #7 was rescheduled to follow Bumper #8, the last rocket in the test series. Bumper #8 was launched on July 24, 1950 from virgin Launch Pad 3. This was the first launch from Cape Canaveral. Bumper #7 eventually flew on July 29, 1950 in the second launch from the Cape.

LARK

Classification: Surface-to-Air Missile

Length: 13 Feet, 11 Inches

Diameter: 18 Inches

Wingspan: 6 Feet, 2 Inches

Finspan: 4 Feet

Range: 30 Miles

Date of First Cape Canaveral Launch: October 25, 1950

Date of Final Cape Canaveral Launch: July 8, 1953

Number of Cape Canaveral Launches: 40

Lark missile development began in 1944 by the U.S. Navy. The missile was designed to be launched from ships against Japanese Kamikaze aircraft. Development contracts were assigned to Fairchild and Consolidated Vultee Aircraft. Flight tests of the missile were not begun until 1946, a year after the close of World War II. Although it was an effective anti-aircraft missile, the Lark program was canceled in 1950.

Surplus Lark missiles were launched from Cape Canaveral, primarily for troop training in missile handling and to test components for more advanced missile programs. Lark missiles were launched and flown employing a booster and sustainer engine. A solid-fueled rocket provided liftoff thrust while a Reaction Motors liquid-fueled sustainer engine provided flight power. Each Lark missile carried a 100-pound high explosive charge, which was detonated by proximity fuse.

MATADOR

Classification: Surface-to-Surface Cruise Missile

Length: 39 feet, 7 inches

Diameter: 4 feet, 6 inches

Wingspan: 28 feet, 8 inches

Range: 500 miles

Date of First Cape Canaveral Launch: June 20, 1951

Date of Final Cape Canaveral Launch: June 1, 1961

Number of Cape Canaveral Launches: 286

Specifications for the Matador pilotless bomber, originally designated XB-61, were drafted in August, 1945, just prior to the conclusion of World War II.

Although a need for the missile was not considered as critical following the war, a limited development contract was issued to Glenn L. Martin Company (later Martin Marietta) in 1946.

Priority and production of the Matador was stepped up in 1950 as a result of the Korean War. A Matador production vehicle designated B-61A, later TM-61A, was approved by the U.S. Air Force in January, 1951 at which time production of the missile officially began.

On October 1, 1951 the U.S. Air Force activated the First Pilotless Bomber Squadron (Light) at Patrick Air Force Base, Florida. On January 10, 1952 the U.S. Air Force followed up with the activation of the 69th Pilotless Bomber Squadron (Light).

These were the first units of their kind in the history of the U.S. Air Force, with operational training conducted by the 6555th Guided Missile Wing at Patrick Air Force Base, Florida. Initially, this training was so secret that some military personnel involved in the program were "officially" assigned to the base as cooks.

On January 15, 1954 the operational units were transferred to the Tactical Air Command to be made combat ready. The First Pilotless Bomber Squadron was subsequently deployed in West Germany, while the 69th Pilotless Bomber Squadron was split and deployed in Formosa and Orlando, Florida.

The Matador could carry a 3,000-pound conventional or nuclear warhead, and was designed to be launched

4

from either a mobile ramp or hardened shelter.

A 50,000-pound launch thrust was provided by a solid-fueled booster attached under the Matador's tail. Cruise thrust of 4,600 pounds was provided by a turbojet engine.

The earliest Matador required line-of-sight radio guidance, which substantially decreased its desired 650-mile range.

An upgraded Matador, designated TM-61B, added a Shanicle hyperbolic guidance system which increased the missile's range to a maximum of 500 miles.

About 1,000 Matador missiles were ultimately carried in the U.S. Air Force inventory.

SNARK

Classification: Surface-to-Surface Cruise Missile

Length: 75 feet, 11 inches

Diameter: 4 feet, 6 inches

Wingspan: 42 feet, 3 inches

Range: 6,325 miles

Date of First Cape Canaveral Launch: August 29, 1952

Date of Final Cape Canaveral Launch: December 5, 1960

Number of Cape Canaveral Launches: 97

Although the program was relatively short-lived, the Snark held the distinction of becoming the first operational U.S. intercontinental missile. The Snark also played an important role in the development of launch facilities and infrastructure at Cape Canaveral.

Like the Atlas ICBM, the Snark cruise missile was born in October, 1945. At the time, the U.S. military began exploring several options for delivering nuclear weapons payloads over vast distances using unmanned vehicles.

A development contract for a long-range winged cruise missile was awarded to prime contractor Northrup in January, 1946. However, budget restraints did not allow an early test version of the Snark, designated N-25, to fly until 1951.

Nevertheless, development of the Snark progressed quickly. By the time an operational prototype of the Snark, designated N-69, was test flown for the first time on August 6, 1953, the missile's range and payload had been doubled over specifications originally envisioned.

As the Snark continued to prove itself during flight testing, a high priority was placed on the program. It was not until 1954 that the U.S. determined that ballistic missiles could carry nuclear weapons between continents. This afforded the Snark a developmental edge.

Alternately referred to as a pilotless bomber, the Snark cruise missile, designated SM-62A, had a large fuselage which could carry 26,000 pounds of liquid fuel.

The Snark was powered in flight by a turbojet which could produce a 10,500-pound thrust. A Nortronics stellar inertial guidance system, using a star tracker, controlled the missile. This was the first time a guidance system of this type was employed on a missile.

Although the Snark was originally designed to be carried into field operations by aircraft, this proved to be impractical. The missile itself weighed 15 tons, and required a portable launcher platform that had 16 wheels. This made only land transportation feasible.

Launches could be achieved just one hour after the Snark arrived at a suitable site. From its platform, zero-length launches were achieved by firing two solid-fueled boosters attached to the Snark. Each booster could produce a thrust of 130,000 pounds.

Once these boosters were fired, the Snark began a smooth climb. After climbing steeply for about 50 seconds, the Snark leveled off for a high-altitude cruise at a speed of over 600 m.p.h.

The star tracker provided constant position updates to the stellar inertial guidance system, which was designed to place the Snark on a ballistic trajectory toward its target.

Upon approach, a warhead was ejected from the main body, and continued to fall toward its target. Once the warhead was ejected, the main body of the Snark pitched upward violently and broke up.

The Snark could carry a nuclear payload of up to 20 megatons, and could approach its target from any direction at any height within its operational limits. The missile could also take evasive action without losing guidance accuracy.

But perhaps the most remarkable feature of the Snark was its ability to fly missions of up to 11 hours and return for a landing. Since the Snark was only destroyed if its warhead needed to impact a target, the missile itself could be flown again and again as conditions warranted.

Although it did not employ landing gear, the Snark was able to safely skid to a landing on any flat, level surface. Indeed, many Snark missiles made successful landings at Cape Canaveral, the first missiles to be recovered at the Cape in this way.

It is perhaps the most enduring legacy of the Snark that to this day, the runway at Cape Canaveral is still referred to as the "skid strip" in memory of the Snark missiles that "skidded" along its surface many years ago.

Snark missiles, by then re-designated N-69E, were declared operational in April, 1957 for the 556th Strategic Missile Squadron activated at Patrick Air Force Base, just south of the Cape. The squadron was later deployed at Presque Isle, Maine.

This lone Snark squadron was renamed the 702nd Strategic Missile Squadron in July, 1959. In 1961, the squadron was deactivated as Snark missiles were withdrawn from service in the wake of the Atlas ICBM.

With an operational life of only four years, the Snark still remains one of the best remembered programs in the history of the Cape. Not only will the "skid strip" name endure in honor of the missile, so will tales of "Snark infested waters" stemming from Snark failures.

While the term may not do justice to what was an advanced cruise missile in its day, references to "Snark infested waters" remain one of the best known anecdotal ties to the history of early operations at Cape Canaveral.

BOMARC A

Classification: Surface-to-Air Cruise Missile

Length: 45 feet, 3 inches

Diameter: 2 feet, 11 inches

Wingspan: 18 feet, 2 inches

Range: 230 miles

Date of First Cape Canaveral Launch: September 10, 1952

Date of Final Cape Canaveral Launch: April 21, 1959

Number of Cape Canaveral Launches: 63

Following initial research and development activities after World War II, the pilotless interceptor aircraft or Surface-to-Air Missile (SAM) was envisioned as an instant readiness supersonic cruise aircraft with a range of several hundred miles.

The SAM concept was created primarily to protect the U.S. mainland from enemy aircraft. By 1949, the first SAM designs were presented to the U.S. Air Force for consideration. These included plans for the Bomarc.

The Bomarc name was derived directly from its creators. Boeing designed the vehicle in association with the University of Michigan Aeronautical Research Center.

Hence, the "BOeing Michigan Aeronautical Research Center" entry into SAM development was born.

Boeing was granted a full contract for Bomarc production in 1951 under the XF-99 designation. The numerical designation would eventually change to IM-99A and CIM-10A.

The first production vehicle became known as Bomarc A, while a more advanced version became known as the Bomarc B.

Bomarc incorporated a basic airplane configuration with an advanced airframe designed to endure vertical take-off and cruising speed in excess of four times the speed of sound.

The wing tips were cropped, and could pivot to act as ailerons. Bomarc also incorporated a fin, the tip of which acted as a rudder. In addition, the tailplanes acted as elevators. The total package made the Bomarc a very reliable cruise missile.

Two body pylons carried underneath the wings each housed a Marquardt ramjet engine capable of producing 10,000 pounds of thrust.

At launch, the vehicle was powered by an Aerojet-General motor with a gimbaled chamber. This motor was fueled by acid/JP-4 liquid propellant.

A few seconds after launch, the Marquardt ramjets, fueled by 80 octane gasoline, fired and the Bomarc aerodynamic components were activated.

Bomarc was the first weapons system to employ an active homing system. Interceptions were controlled by a Semi-Automatic Ground Environment (SAGE) system designed to alert and control the SAM toward its target.

In 1958, Bomarc guidance was improved to include Back-Up Interceptor Control (BUIC), creating a more reliable SAGE/BUIC interceptor combination.

The Bomarc was designed to be housed in shelters having a roof that could split right and left down the middle, allowing the missile to be raised prior to a quick launch.

While this type of shelter was used initially, the structures proved to be too expensive to construct and maintain. As a result, later Bomarc facilities employed a more simple shelter with a sliding roof.

Originally, the Bomarc could be launched within two minutes following a target alert. The launch time was later reduced to just 30 seconds.

The missile could cruise at 65,000 feet as it headed toward its target. About 10 miles from the target, the SAGE or SAGE/BUIC control was cut out, and a Westinghouse radar located in the nose of the Bomarc A guided the vehicle to target impact.

The Bomarc could be fitted with a conventional explosive or nuclear weapons payload.

A Bomarc missile prototype was first test-flown on September 10, 1952. The operational version was ready for its first test flight by February, 1955.

On October 2, 1957, a Bomarc A launched from Cape Canaveral successfully flew to within lethal distance of a drone Navaho X-10 test vehicle flying nearly twice the speed of sound at an altitude of 48,000 feet.

Remarkably, this Bomarc mission employed a SAGE interceptor system controlled from Kingston, New York. Of course, the valuable Navaho X-10 target vehicle was never destroyed during the test and made a successful return flight to Cape Canaveral.

Boeing began delivering operational Bomarc missiles to the U.S. Air Force in 1957, with a total of 366 deployed by 1960 at bases which could house one or two 28-missile squadrons.

Initially, Bomarc A deployment occurred at Dow Air Force Base, Maine, Otis Air Force Base, Massachusetts, McGuire Air Force Base, New Jersey and Suffolk Air Force Base, New York.

RV-A-10

Classification: Research Rocket

Length: 20 feet, 3 inches

Finspan: 7 feet, 11 inches

Diameter: 31 inches

Date of First Cape Canaveral Launch: February 11, 1953

Date of Final Cape Canaveral Launch: March 25, 1953

Number of Cape Canaveral Launches: 4

RV-A-10 was a research rocket built for the U.S. Army Project Hermes. The rocket was designed to test the feasibility of large, solid-fueled rocket engines. It was powered by a Thiokol solid-fuel engine capable of producing a liftoff thrust of 32,000 pounds. The RV-A-10 could reach a maximum altitude of 36 miles with a maximum range of 68 miles. Test launches confirmed that large, solid-fueled rocket engines were feasible and could be employed in future rockets and missiles.

REDSTONE

Classification: Medium-Range Ballistic Missile

Length: 69 feet

Diameter: 5 feet, 10 inches

Finspan: 13 feet

Range: 200 miles

Date of First Cape Canaveral Launch: August 20, 1953

Date of Final Cape Canaveral Launch: June 26, 1961

Number of Cape Canaveral Launches: 27

Not only did the Redstone hold the distinction of being the first operational U.S. ballistic missile, it also played a pivotal role in the birth of America's space program.

The Redstone missile was originally a product of the U.S. Army Ordnance Guided Missile Center (OGMC) based at the Redstone Arsenal in Huntsville, Alabama.

The outbreak of the Korean War in 1950 coupled with a growing concern over ballistic missile advances by the Soviet Union spearheaded the development of a more advanced version of the German V-2.

Since nuclear warheads were still relatively heavy at the time, the Redstone missile was designed to carry a 6,000-pound warhead a distance of 500 miles.

The range was later reduced to 200 miles to allow the application of existing Navaho missile engine technology. The Navaho engines reduced the range of the Redstone, but facilitated quicker development.

In 1950, a team of German scientists led by Wernher von Braun was re-assigned to OGMC at Huntsville. Previously, the von Braun team had been based at Fort Bliss, Texas and White Sands, New Mexico.

This transfer was an important one for von Braun. Not only did the scientist have a chance to help develop a viable U.S. weapons program, he also was able to fulfill a personal dream of designing rockets which would carry satellites and men into space.

The Redstone would prove to be instrumental in both efforts.

Initially designated Missile M-8 under Weapons System SSM-A-14, the Redstone was built as a field-mobile missile capable of being launched by combat troops. The Redstone was later redesignated PGM-11A.

North American Aviation produced the Redstone engine, which was directly adapted from the Navaho cruise missile. The engine burned a combination of liquid oxygen and a liquid fuel which was 75 percent ethyl alcohol and 25 percent water.

The Redstone engine produced 77,200 pounds of thrust at liftoff utilizing a 780-horsepower turbopump with a precision cutoff mechanism. Trajectory was controlled by four vanes which were attached to four fixed fins at the base of the missile.

Each fin supported a single moveable vane each. The vanes moved on pivots which were attached to the inside face of each fin. The vanes deflected the engine's exhaust to steer the missile. This was a method nearly identical to that employed on the German V-2.

Prior to launch, the Redstone was supported on a circular stand. A cone-shaped flame deflector was located directly beneath the stand. The flame deflector helped to keep the missile stable when its engine was fired.

Following launch, the Redstone was controlled by an inertial guidance system built by the Ford Instrument Division of Sperry Rand. The system used air-breathing gyroscopes. The re-entry vehicle, carrying a nuclear weapon, separated from the missile following engine cutoff.

The first Redstone was test launched from Cape Canaveral Launch Pad 4 on August 20, 1953. After numerous test flights, the Redstone was declared operational in June, 1958.

The ABMA granted a Redstone production contract to Chrysler, and over 1,000 missiles were delivered. Contrary to procedures adopted by the U.S. Air Force, the ABMA fabricated and tested the Redstone in-house prior to issuing a production contract.

The Redstone was deployed by Field Artillery Missile Groups (FAMG) in West Germany. Comprised of about 600 people and many large vehicles, each FAMG had to operate a liquid oxygen processing plant which could yield 20 short-tons of the liquid fuel per day.

ABMA development and testing of the Pershing missile began at about the same time the Redstone was declared operational. Work on the Pershing progressed very quickly, and it replaced all Redstone missiles in the field by 1963.

Although it had an operational life of only five years, the Redstone remains one of the single most important vehicles in the history of the U.S. space program.

The Redstone was used as a first stage booster for the Jupiter C research rocket, which was later renamed Juno I and carried the first U.S. satellite, Explorer I, into orbit on January 31, 1958.

In addition, the Redstone was adapted by NASA in an effort to launch the first U.S. astronauts. A modified Redstone missile, mated to a Mercury capsule, successfully carried Alan Shepard, the first American astronaut, into space on May 5, 1961.

Although the Redstone was only powerful enough to support sub-orbital manned flights, the vehicle did repeat its historic task as Virgil "Gus" Grissom flew aboard a Mercury Redstone on July 21, 1961.

As a follow-up to the Redstone program, the ABMA continued development of the Juno family of space launch vehicles. With the Redstone as the basis of the first generation Juno I, additional versions to Juno V were designed.

The final generation, called Juno V, was to employ a first stage array of eight Redstone missile stages clustered around one central Jupiter missile stage. Although the Juno rocket family was renamed Saturn, the Saturn I bore great resemblance to the proposed Juno V.

In essence, the Saturn rockets which were instrumental in the effort to carry the first men to the Moon were direct descendants of the Redstone vehicles which had already triumphantly carried the first U.S. satellite and the first U.S. astronaut into space.

X-17

Classification: Research Rocket

Length: 40 feet, 6 inches

Finspan: 8 feet, 6 inches

Date of First Cape Canaveral Launch: May 23, 1955

Date of Final Cape Canaveral Launch: March 21, 1957

Number of Cape Canaveral Launches: 37

Although relatively short-lived, the X-17 research rocket played a vital role in U.S. ballistic missile and nuclear weapons development.

The X-17 program was born in 1954 as military officials realized that no hard data was available on how missile nose cones would react during high-speed re-entry through Earth's atmosphere.

At a time when ICBM development was about to reach fever pitch, a research rocket was needed to help determine the best shape, size and aerodynamic characteristics of re-entry vehicles which would be used to deliver a nuclear weapons payload to its target.

The U.S. Air Force granted a contract to Lockheed in January, 1955 to develop a rocket capable of gathering data on nose cone performance during actual flight conditions.

Development of the resulting X-17 rocket occurred very quickly. On May 8, 1955 the first of three 1/4-scale versions of the X-17 was delivered to Cape Canaveral for flight testing.

These 1/4-scale vehicles were used to test flight support hardware as well as anticipate aerodynamic performance of the proposed full-scale version of the X-17.

With the "Q" standing for "Quarter", the 1/4-scale versions of the X-17 were named Q-1, Q-2 and Q-3. Q-1 and Q-2 each employed a solid-fueled rocket as a first stage and carried non-separable wooden dummy second and third stages.

Q-1 and Q-2 were both launched on May 23, 1955. While very little data was acquired during these flights, the X-17 support team did gain necessary operational experience.

Q-3 employed a solid-fueled rocket as a first stage which could actually separate from its two dummy upper stages. Designed to achieve this separation in actual flight conditions, Q-3 exploded just three seconds after its launch on June 13, 1955.

These 1/4-scale flights were followed by a series of test launches featuring three 1/2-scale versions off the X-17. These flights were intended to verify data acquired during the 1/4-scale tests.

Numbered H-1, H-2 and H-3, with the "H" standing for "Half", all three 1/2-scale versions of the X-17 employed a solid-fueled rocket as a first stage, three solid-fueled NOTS rockets as a second stage and a single solid-fueled NOTS rocket as a third stage.

H-1, H-2 and H-3 were launched on June 23, 1955, June 30, 1955 and July 14, 1955, respectively. Stability of these 1/2-scale rockets was very poor during flight, and each one reached less than half of the velocity anticipated.

Nevertheless, enough data was acquired during the 1/4-scale and 1/2-scale X-17 test flights to justify pressing ahead with test flights of the full-scale version.

A series of full-scale developmental flights was planned to test, and if necessary correct, overall X-17 vehicle performance prior to the start of operational research missions.

The first six full-scale versions of the X-17 were numbered D-1 through D-6, with the "D" standing for "Development". All of the X-17 rockets which followed were numbered beginning with R-1, with the "R" standing for "Research".

Test flights of the developmental versions of the full-scale X-17 began on August 26, 1955 and concluded on June 26, 1956. Early in this series, problems were encountered regarding second and third stage performance.

These problems were ironed out through component testing at Holloman Air Force Base, New Mexico. As a precautionary measure, a decision was made to use the first scheduled operational research version of the X-17, called R-1, for a developmental test flight on April 17, 1956.

Operational research flights of the X-17 began on July 17, 1956 with the launch of rocket R-2.

The full-scale X-17 employed three solid-fueled stages. The first stage was powered by a Thiokol Sergeant rocket which could produce a thrust of 48,000 pounds.

The second stage employed three Thiokol Recruit rockets which could each produce a thrust of 33,900 pounds. The third stage was powered by a single Thiokol Recruit rocket which could produce a 35,950-pound thrust by utilizing an enlarged exhaust nozzle.

Two small solid-fueled spin-stabilization motors were strapped to the first stage. Ignited at launch, these motors were jettisoned just a few seconds later.

X-17 rockets were transported to the launch site on a specially designed trailer/erector. After the rocket was elevated to a vertical launch position by two hydraulic actuators, the trailer was removed.

The first stage of the X-17 carried the rocket to an altitude of about 90,000 feet before expending its fuel and shutting down. Using its own momentum, the X-17 continued to a maximum altitude of about 500,000 feet.

Once peak altitude was reached, the X-17 began an uncontrolled fall toward Earth. At an altitude between 90,000 feet and 70,000 feet, a pressure sensor located on the X-17 fins activated an explosive device which separated the rocket's first stage.

About a second later, the second stage was fired. It burned less than two seconds prior to ignition of the third stage, which also burned less than two seconds. Despite these short bursts, tremendous speed was achieved during this re-entry process.

Speeds approaching 10,000 m.p.h. were reached during the flight of an X-17, which typically lasted six minutes and covered a distance of about 135 miles.

During re-entry, valuable data was transmitted from test nose cones regarding temperature, pressure and flight dynamics. X-17 rockets flew with nose cones of differing shapes, including hemisphere, cubic paraboloid and blunt.

A total of 25 operational research X-17 flights were conducted through July 22, 1957. Results of these flights were mixed, but the X-17 served the pivotal role of determining that blunt nose cones provided the best shape for use on both the Atlas and Titan ICBM.

In 1958, seven additional X-17 rockets were manufactured for Project Argus, an ambitious program conducted to detonate nuclear weapons payloads at altitudes greater than 300 miles. X-17 rockets used for Project Argus were specially modified for this task.

Project Argus launches of X-17 rockets were conducted from the ship U.S.S. Norton Sound in the summer and fall of 1958. Four test launches occurred off San Clemente, California. These were followed by three live nuclear detonations over the South Pacific.

NAVAHO X-10

Classification: Surface-to-Surface Cruise Missile Prototype

Length: 87 feet, 4 inches

Wingspan: 40 feet, 3 inches

Diameter: 6 feet

Date of First Cape Canaveral Launch: August 19, 1955

Date of Final Cape Canaveral Launch: January 26, 1959

Number of Cape Canaveral Launches: 15

The Navaho program was born in 1947 as part of a plan to create an unmanned winged cruise missile which could fly a desired range of 5,500 miles.

Considered the most advanced aircraft under design at the time, a contract for production and testing of Navaho missiles was granted to North American Aviation.

The first version of the Navaho was designated the Navaho X-10. The X-10 series was produced to test the missile's canard aerodynamics, flight control system, inertial guidance, advanced honeycomb structure plus new materials and equipment.

The recoverable Navaho X-10 carried retractable landing gear, and was launched like a conventional aircraft. Navaho X-10 vehicles were launched from the skid strip at Cape Canaveral. Upon completing their test flights, the vehicles simply flew back for a landing.

Following cancellation of the Navaho program, surplus X-10 vehicles were used as target drones during surface-to-air missile tests. The re-useable X-10 vehicles were, of course, not destroyed during these missions and returned for a landing as designed.

JUPITER A

Classification: Research Rocket

Length: 69 feet

Diameter: 5 feet, 10 inches

Finspan: 13 feet

Date of First Cape Canaveral Launch: March 14, 1956

Date of Final Cape Canaveral Launch: January 14, 1958

Number of Cape Canaveral Launches: 20

The Jupiter A was the first adaptation of the Redstone MRBM used for testing certain components which would be incorporated into the Jupiter IRBM.

Although it could correctly be classified as a Redstone, the Army Ballistic Missile Agency (ABMA) named the vehicle Jupiter A to more closely associate it with its Jupiter missile development program.

This was primarily due to increasing competition for launch dates at Cape Canaveral. Out of necessity, certain programs were given priority over others when launch dates were selected.

For a time, nearly the highest priority was given to Jupiter-related test flights. For this reason, the name Jupiter A more precisely identified the purpose of the vehicle, and guaranteed a much higher scheduling priority than an ordinary Redstone might have received.

With the exception of its name, the Jupiter A was identical to the Redstone MRBM. In fact, Jupiter A flights served an important dual purpose. In addition to serving as a test vehicle for Jupiter missile hardware, Jupiter A flights yielded valuable information on Redstone missile performance. At the time, Redstone was still in the development stage and had yet to be deployed.

JUPITER C

Classification: Research Rocket

Length: 68 feet, 7 inches (Carrying Inert Fourth Stage)

Length: 66 feet, 4 inches (Carrying 1/3-Scale Jupiter Nose Cone)

Diameter: 5 feet, 10 inches

Finspan: 13 feet

Date of First Cape Canaveral Launch: September 20, 1956

Date of Final Cape Canaveral Launch: August 8, 1957

Number of Cape Canaveral Launches: 3

Adapted from the Redstone MRBM as a follow-up to the Jupiter A, the Jupiter C rocket was developed as a test vehicle to evaluate Jupiter IRBM nosecone technology, including various shapes, sizes and materials.

In 1955, a rocket nearly identical to Jupiter C was detailed in Project Orbiter, a joint Army/Office of Naval Research plan for launching satellites during the International Geophysical Year. When Project Orbiter was rejected in favor of Project Vanguard, the multi-stage Redstone concept could well have died.

Project Orbiter was officially rejected on September 9, 1955. However, on September 13, 1955 Secretary of Defense Charles E. Wilson authorized the Army and the Navy to cooperate in the development of the Jupiter IRBM. Just days after the cancellation of Project Orbiter, a multi-stage Redstone was given a new lease on life.

Engineers at the Ordnance Guided Missile Center at the Redstone Arsenal were quickly given authority to develop the Jupiter C to facilitate high-altitude re-entry tests of Jupiter missile components. The work was assumed by the Army Ballistic Missile Agency (ABMA) upon its creation on February 1, 1956.

Like the Jupiter A, the Jupiter C could have been correctly called a Redstone, but the name was changed to Jupiter C, or "Jupiter Composite", short for "Jupiter Composite Re-entry Test Vehicle."

Again, a name tying the vehicle directly to the Jupiter IRBM development program assured the Army very high priority when scheduling launch dates at Cape Canaveral.

The Jupiter C rocket was quite similar to the Juno I as previously described. There were, however, several important differences. The Jupiter C was designed specifically to carry a nosecone into space and allow it to complete a high-speed re-entry.

Both Juno I and Jupiter C employed a Redstone missile as first stage booster, using Redstone tankage extended a total of 96 inches to hold more fuel. However, the Jupiter C Redstone booster burned liquid oxygen and alcohol, like the production version of the Redstone MRBM.

The satellite-bearing Juno I Redstone first stage engine was modified to burn higher energy Hydyne liquid fuel instead of alcohol. Both the Jupiter C and Juno I employed 11 clustered Thiokol Baby Sergeant solid rocket motors as second stage, and three clustered Thiokol Baby Sergeant solid rocket motors as third stage.

Like the Juno I, the Jupiter C clustered second and third stages were housed inside a distinctive rotating "tub", spin-stabilized at several hundred revolutions per minute (actual spin rate depended on the weight of the payload) during ascent. This rotating motion was designed to stabilize the upper stages during flight.

However, since the Jupiter C was not intended to carry satellites into space, it never employed an operational fourth stage motor. Hence, it was a three-stage version of the Redstone, while Juno I was a four-stage version of the Redstone.

The Jupiter C first stage, with a liftoff thrust of 78,000 pounds, burned for 150 seconds after launch, boosting the upper stages to near-space. After first stage cutoff and separation, the clustered upper stages were able to continue an unpowered ballistic flight until reaching the highest altitude momentum would allow.

The second stage was then fired for six seconds, moving quickly away from the rotating "tub" assembly. After second stage cutoff and a two second pause to allow safe stage separation, the third stage was fired for six seconds. It then separated from the payload, which continued a ballistic path toward ultimate ocean impact.

Intense heat was created during re-entry, allowing valuable scientific data on flight dynamics and nosecone performance to be gathered. This aided in the selection and development of the actual nose cones which would be carried aboard operational Jupiter missiles.

From the outset of the Jupiter C program, ABMA made a practice of painting large black letters on the mostly white rocket. These were intended to preserve secrecy about the total number of Redstone boosters being produced.

A numerical value was given to letters in the name Huntsville, where ABMA was based. The numerical code was:

$$H = 1, U = 2, N = 3, T = 4, S = 5, V = 6, I = 7, L = 8, E = 9, X = 0$$

Since the first Jupiter C rocket employed Redstone booster #27, this rocket was painted with a large "UI" as per this established code. The first Jupiter C was launched from Cape Canaveral Launch Pad 5 on September 20, 1956. It performed far beyond expectations.

This Jupiter C was the only one to carry an inert fourth stage motor ballasted with sand lest ABMA "accidentally" launch a satellite before Project Vanguard. The inert fourth stage motor reached a maximum altitude of 682 miles and distance of 3,350 miles, establishing Cape Canaveral records for both altitude and distance.

This was both a blessing and a curse for ABMA, which had effectively demonstrated that the Jupiter C possessed the performance necessary to carry a small satellite into space. However, ABMA remained strictly forbidden to launch a satellite, and would have to impatiently wait almost 16 months for an historic opportunity to do so.

The next Jupiter C, bearing the letters "NT" (Redstone #34) was launched from Cape Canaveral Launch Pad 6 on May 15, 1957. It carried a one-third scale Jupiter "ablative-type" nosecone instead of an inert fourth stage motor.

Although it was intended to be recovered at sea, the nosecone was lost. Due to a guidance programming error, the upper stages fired in the wrong direction. The third stage also failed to separate from the payload.

Nevertheless, performance of this Jupiter C was impressive. The payload, even attached to the third stage, reached a maximum altitude of 354 miles, eventually impacting the ocean 689 miles downrange. The nose cone could not be recovered due to an impact 365 miles short of the target area coupled with recovery system failure.

The third and last Jupiter C, bearing the letters "TX" (Redstone #40) was launched from Cape Canaveral Launch Pad 6 on August 8, 1957. This Jupiter C also carried a one-third scale Jupiter "ablative-type" nose cone, and marked an important "first" for rocketry.

Even though the third stage initially failed to separate from the payload, it did break free during the harsh conditions of re-entry. The nose cone achieved a maximum altitude of 300 miles and impacted the ocean 1,160 miles downrange.

The nose cone was successfully recovered, marking the first time an object was recovered after flying in space. The nose cone was found to be in excellent condition, proving that "ablative-type" nose cones were suitable for deployment aboard Jupiter missiles.

Much to the surprise of ABMA commander Major General J.B. Medaris, the nose cone contained a "rocket-mail" letter to him from Dr. Kurt Debus, director of the ABMA Missile Firing Laboratory at Cape Canaveral.

Medaris accepted the letter and later loaned it to the Smithsonian Institution. But, due to subsequent clandestine efforts of Cape workers to enclose all manner of "rocketmail" in recoverable nose cones, "rocketmail" was banned with threat of severe punishment.

Although a total of 12 Jupiter C rockets had been authorized for construction, Jupiter C research flights were concluded after just three launches. Subsequent wise directives by Medaris would prove vital to a U.S. presence in space.

On August 21, 1957 Medaris canceled the Jupiter C research program and ordered that all remaining Jupiter C booster hardware be placed in protective storage. The move was clearly aimed at storing hardware that could be called upon at a future date to launch satellites.

Medaris was even able to consign and hold the necessary upper stage hardware as part of a "long-term life test" reportedly intended to determine the useful life of the upper stage solid fuel motors.

The specific intent of Medaris was to keep the Jupiter C components in the most advanced state of readiness available to attempt the first launching of a satellite not more than four months from the date authorization was given, followed by additional satellite launchings spaced about one month apart thereafter.

The Army, with Jupiter C performance data in hand, continued to request permission to attempt the launching of instrumented satellites to augment International Geophysical Year scientific research. These requests were consistently denied.

The Soviet launch of Sputnik I, the world's first artificial satellite, coupled with persistent problems in Project

Vanguard would have a profound effect on the future of the Jupiter C rocket and U.S. satellite efforts.

Purely by chance, ABMA officials were entertaining Secretary of Defense Neil McElroy at the Redstone Arsenal on October 4, 1957, the day Sputnik I was launched. An impromptu effort was immediately made to convince McElroy that ABMA deserved a chance to launch satellites.

Secret directives by Medaris would follow soon afterward, as Wernher von Braun, Technical Director of ABMA, was instructed to begin preparing Jupiter C hardware for the launching of satellites. Discussions were also initiated with the Army-sponsored Jet Propulsion Laboratory to evaluate the specific design of satellites.

Secretary of Defense McElroy did convince President Eisenhower that ABMA deserved consideration to launch satellites, but it would be almost two months after the launch of Sputnik I before ABMA was granted official authorization to schedule and stick with satellite launch dates.

Prior overtures made to ABMA regarding the launching of satellites had hinged on the outcome of Project Vanguard attempts, with no guarantees that ABMA satellite programs would not be canceled abruptly if Project Vanguard scored an early success. This issue was resolved by late November, 1957 and ABMA was given a firm order to proceed.

As it turned out, Project Vanguard would play into the hands of ABMA in a big way. The first Project Vanguard attempt to launch a small, grapefruit-sized tracking satellite met with failure. Vanguard rocket TV-3 exploded on Cape Canaveral Launch Pad 18A on December 6, 1957.

As fate would have it, ABMA would now get the first crack at launching the first U.S. satellite. The first ABMA satellite launch attempt had been scheduled for January 29, 1958. This was originally slated to be five days after the second Project Vanguard satellite launch attempt.

However, delays associated with Project Vanguard caused their target launch date to slip to early February, 1958. If ABMA could prepare their launch vehicle and satellite payload as planned, they would get the opportunity they had long coveted.

Jupiter C processing was going smoothly due to the earlier directives by Medaris, but a major change was in store for the rocket. On November 18, 1957 Dr. William Pickering, head of the Jet Propulsion Laboratory, suggested to Medaris that the satellite-bearing version of the Jupiter C be renamed Juno.

The recommendation was accepted by ABMA, and the Juno family of rockets was born. Indeed, a Juno I rocket bearing the letters "UE" (Redstone #29) would successfully launch the first U.S. satellite, Explorer I, at 10:48 p.m. EST on January 31, 1958.

It should be noted that although the Jupiter C rocket had been renamed Juno I prior to the launch of Explorer I, many books and documents, especially those published just after the historic launch, refer to the Explorer I launch vehicle as a Jupiter C.

Purists may continue to argue merits for the use of either name, but the plain fact is that both Jupiter C and Juno I were actually multi-stage Redstones!

NAVAHO XSM-64

Classification: Surface-to-Surface Cruise Missile

Length With Booster: 95 feet, 3 inches

Length Without Booster: 87 feet, 4 inches

Wingspan: 40 feet, 3 inches

Diameter: 6 feet

Range: 6,325 miles

Date of First Cape Canaveral Launch: November 6, 1956

Date of Final Cape Canaveral Launch: November 18, 1958

Number of Cape Canaveral Launches: 11

The production version of the Navaho missile was designated the Navaho XSM-64. It was comparable to an actual bomber, and could fly at a speed of 2,150 m.p.h. at a maximum altitude of 60,000 feet.

Remarkably, the Navaho XSM-64 was heavier than the heaviest airliners flying at the time.

It was launched at a 90-degree angle attached to a cylindrical booster. Three engines at the base of the booster were fed by liquid oxygen/RP-1 (kerosene) liquid fuel. These engines produced a combined 450,000-pound thrust at launch.

After a vertical climb, the Navaho XSM-64 arched over. Twin on-board ramjets were ignited as the vehicle and booster package separated. The missile then flew on to its target.

Designed to be re-used following non-lethal flights, Navaho XSM-64 vehicles also carried retractable landing gear and were able to return for a landing.

Although able to demonstrate innovative and ambitious technology, the Navaho program was cancelled in July, 1957.

The cancellation was primarily due to advances in ICBM technology, which made the Navaho redundant and therefore unnecessary as a vehicle designed to hit targets over 6,000 miles away.

Navaho test flights continued following the cancellation, although most of the Navaho XSM-64 test flights resulted in the accidental destruction of the vehicles.

However, the Navaho series concluded with a successful test flight on November 18, 1958. Despite its short life, the Navaho remains an important vehicle in the history of the U.S. missile and space program.

Navaho technology, including booster engines, cryogenic propellant, inertial guidance systems and other equipment was successfully adapted for use in other missile programs.

In fact, the pump-fed Navaho booster engine technology, itself adapted from the German V-2 missile, was directly applied to the Atlas, Redstone, Jupiter and Thor programs.

Since these four missiles laid the foundation for generations of space launch vehicles which sent men to the Moon and continue to carry satellites into space, the Navaho missile deserves a special place of honor despite the fact it was never operationally deployed.

The last Navaho XSM-64 missile known to exist is on permanent display outside the south entrance gate to Cape Canaveral Air Force Station, where it was moved in March, 1999 after undergoing an extensive refurbishing project sponsored by the Air Force Space and Missile Museum.

VANGUARD

Classification: Space Launch Vehicle

Length: 72 feet

Diameter: 3 feet, 9 inches

Date of First Cape Canaveral Launch: December 8, 1956

Date of Final Cape Canaveral Launch: September 18, 1959

Number Launched from Cape Canaveral: 14

Vanguard was the first U.S. rocket designed for the specific purpose of launching satellites, and represented the first program on Cape Canaveral that was not tied to a weapons system. The rocket was intended to launch the first U.S. satellite, and although it was never able to fulfill this objective, Vanguard remains a vital element in the genesis of the U.S. space program.

In March, 1955 the Eisenhower Administration approved a plan to orbit a series of instrumented Earth satellites during the International Geophysical Year (IGY) which extended from July 1, 1957 through December 31, 1958. The IGY was an unprecedented international effort to advance scientific studies of Earth.

With U.S. rocket research still in a state of relative infancy, a decision on what sort of rockets and satellites would be launched was delegated to Assistant Secretary of Defense for Research and Development Donald Quarles. Quarles formed the Advisory Group on Special Capabilities to consider available options and render a final determination. This group was nicknamed the Stewart Committee in honor of its chairman, Homer J. Stewart who represented the then Army-sponsored Jet Propulsion Laboratory.

The Stewart Committee was comprised of eight members. Two members represented the Army, two members represented the Navy, two members represented the Air Force and two members were appointed by Quarles. The Stewart Committee began meeting in July, 1955 and was presented with three distinct options.

The first, named Project Orbiter, was a joint Army-Navy proposal which would employ a multi-stage version of the Army's Redstone missile as a booster. The second, ultimately named Vanguard, was a Navy Research Laboratory proposal which would employ a multi-stage version of the Navy's Viking research rocket as a booster. A third proposal was offered by the Air Force, which would employ its yet-to-be-flown Atlas missile as a booster.

On August 3, 1955 the Stewart Committee voted 5 to 2, with one member absent, to select Vanguard to launch a series of IGY satellites. Proponents of Project Orbiter objected bitterly, but the decision of the Stewart Committee was officially endorsed by President Eisenhower and the Department of Defense on September 9, 1955.

Vanguard offered several advantages, including civilian management of booster and satellite development. This reflected a desire of President Eisenhower to distance the military from IGY research efforts. Although the Viking rocket which would provide the core of the Vanguard booster was a product of the Navy, it had been used strictly for scientific purposes.

And, Viking was a proven vehicle. On May 24, 1954 a Viking rocket launched from White Sands, New Mexico successfully carried an 852-pound scientific payload to an altitude of 158 miles, considered to be beyond the threshold of space. Although this was not the first time an object had been sent into space, it did validate the Viking as a reliable scientific platform upon which to build the Vanguard program.

In addition, Vanguard would not draw resources away from vital ballistic missile research being conducted by the Army and Air Force. The decision of the Stewart Committee has, to an extent, been characterized as a bitter rivalry between the Army and Navy. This is not completely accurate, since the Navy in fact provided vital technical support of Redstone-based Project Orbiter. Also, the 5 to 2 vote of the Stewart Committee was clearly not cast along the political lines of any branch of military service, each of which was equally represented.

The Vanguard rocket emerged as a relatively small three-stage vehicle employing a modified Viking rocket as first stage. The first stage engine, manufactured by General Electric, burned a combination of liquid oxygen and RP-1 (kerosene) liquid fuel and could produce a thrust of 28,000 pounds. An Aerojet second stage engine burned IWFNA/UDMH liquid fuel and could produce a 7,500-pound thrust. A solid-fueled Altair third stage produced a thrust of 3,100 pounds. Prime contractor for the Vanguard rocket was the Martin Company.

At least six Vanguard rockets had been scheduled for test launches prior to what would have been the first U.S. attempt to launch a satellite. Since the IGY extended through the end of 1958 and a firm decision in support of Vanguard was made in 1955, it was believed that there was plenty of time for Vanguard to prove itself before attempting the launch of a satellite. However, development problems with Vanguard surfaced quickly, and the first test launch did not occur until December 8, 1956. A second test launch was conducted on May 1, 1957.

Before even a third Vanguard test launch could occur, the Soviet Union shocked the world with their launch of the world's first artificial satellite, Sputnik I, on October 4, 1957. The third Vanguard test launch was conducted about three weeks later on October 23, 1957.

To counter a remarkable and unexpected Soviet achievement, which was followed by their launch of Sputnik II on November 3, 1957 a bold decision was made to attempt a satellite launch aboard the next available Vanguard rocket, a "Test Vehicle" called TV-3. This launch would occur prior to the conclusion of the test series originally intended to validate the Vanguard rocket. TV-3 would be the first Vanguard rocket to fly with powered upper stages, and the success of the mission was doubtful.

Vanguard TV-3, carrying a tiny 3.25-pound, 6.4-inch diameter spherical tracking satellite made of aluminum, exploded on Cape Canaveral Launch Pad 18A just seconds after it was launched on December 6, 1957. The first U.S. attempt to launch a satellite had failed dramatically before the eyes of the world. Subsequent troubleshooting of the Vanguard rocket allowed the Army Ballistic Missile Agency (ABMA) to launch the first U.S. satellite, Explorer I, aboard a four-stage version of the Redstone missile on January 31, 1958. The effort allowed the initially rejected Redstone-based Project Orbiter to be vindicated.

Despite the highly publicized Vanguard failure on December 6, 1957 the Vanguard program continued. A second, but less spectacular, Vanguard failure occurred upon a follow-up satellite launch attempt on February 5, 1958. But success would follow. The next Vanguard rocket carried the Vanguard-1 satellite into orbit on March 17, 1958. This was the second U.S. satellite successfully placed in orbit. Vanguard-1 remains the oldest man-made object in space, expected to orbit Earth for about 1,000 years. Like the payload carried aboard the failed Vanguard TV-3, Vanguard-1 was a 3.25-pound, 6.4-inch diameter aluminum tracking satellite.

The next four attempts to launch satellites aboard Vanguard rockets failed, but the Vanguard-2 satellite was successfully launched on February 17, 1959. After two more Vanguard failures, the very last launch of a Vanguard rocket scored a success. The Vanguard-3 satellite was successfully launched on September 18, 1959. Both Vanguard-2 and Vanguard-3 were instrumented satellites weighing just over 22 pounds.

Although retired after just 14 flights, Vanguard technology was successfully applied to other programs. The rocket's upper stages formed the basis for upper stage configurations employed on Atlas-Able, Thor-Able and Scout rockets. Vanguard technology even found its way into the NASA Apollo program, with a modified Vanguard upper stage forming the basis of the Atlas-Antares second stage. Atlas-Antares was used in NASA Project Fire to test proposed Apollo re-entry vehicle designs.

THOR

Classification: Intermediate-Range Ballistic Missile

Length: 65 feet

Diameter: 8 feet

Range: 1,976 miles

Date of First Cape Canaveral Launch: January 25, 1957

Date of Final Cape Canaveral Launch: July 18, 1962

Number of Cape Canaveral Launches: 51

In addition to giving the U.S. Air Force a potent weapon to augment its ballistic missile arsenal, the Thor IRBM laid an important foundation for the U.S. space program as it formed the basis of the long-lived Delta rocket family.

Development of the Thor was authorized in November, 1955 to give the U.S. Air Force an independent IRBM capability. At the time, the U.S. Army Ballistic Missile Agency (ABMA) was well underway in the development of the Redstone MRBM and Jupiter IRBM.

Since the U.S. Air Force was now authorized to, in effect, compete with the U.S. Army in the development of an IRBM weapons system, a fierce rivalry between these two branches of service erupted.

Although it was designed to be operationally similar to the Jupiter IRBM, the Thor weapons system incorporated fixed service structures in the field. Associated service equipment accounted for 87% of the overall development costs of the Thor.

The Jupiter program was more streamlined and was designed as a fully mobile weapons system with relatively simple launch stands and servicing requirements.

Another striking difference between the Thor and Jupiter concerned the process of producing the missiles. ABMA designed, tested and built their missiles in-house. A production contract was not issued until this entire process was completed and a final design was approved.

In contrast, the U.S. Air Force issued its production contract as soon as a design concept was approved. Design, testing and construction of the vehicles was placed in the hands of the selected contractor.

A complete system contract for the Thor was granted to Douglas Aircraft in December, 1955.

Initially, it was clear that the U.S. Air Force was in a race with ABMA in securing funding for its fledgling IRBM program. Intense and bitter political maneuvers were carried out by each side.

However, the final blow in this conflict was struck fairly early on in the development of the Thor. The 1956 "Wilson Memorandum" issued from the Pentagon stripped the U.S. Army of all missiles with a range of 200 miles or greater.

The U.S. Air Force vigorously pursued its Thor program. ABMA also continued development of the Jupiter, but the U.S. Army would never be able to deploy the missile in the field. Rather, ABMA would act as a contract supplier of Jupiter missiles to the U.S. Air Force.

In effect, the "Wilson Memorandum" authorized the U.S. Air Force to continue the development of two separate IRBM weapons systems.

With some of the intensity in the rivalry between the U.S. Air Force and ABMA thus reduced, the Thor was granted the highest national priority alongside the Atlas ICBM.

Under Weapons System-315A (WS-315A), the Thor was given a numerical designation of SM-75. Final design of the missile was completed in July, 1956. At this time, a production line of Thor prototypes was displayed in the Douglas Aircraft factory in Santa Monica, California.

The first production model of the Thor was delivered to the U.S. Air Force in October, 1956. At just 11 months, this represented the shortest span of time from conception to delivery for any U.S. missile program.

A full two-thirds of the Thor body held liquid fuel for the missile's single-stage engine. A gimbaled Rocketdyne engine, fed by liquid oxygen/RP-1 (kerosene) liquid fuel, could produce 150,000 pounds of thrust at launch.

This thrust capability was similar to both the Jupiter IRBM engine and each individual Atlas ICBM booster stage engine. All of these engines were derived from the Navaho cruise missile program.

Two Rocketdyne vernier engines were attached at opposite sides of the base of the Thor. The vernier engines, similar to those used on the Atlas ICBM, burned the same fuel as the main engine and could each produce a 1,000-pound thrust. They adjusted roll and velocity.

Inertial guidance for the Thor was provided by an AC Sparkplug system utilizing liquid-floated gyroscopes. To save development costs, the Thor carried a copper heat-sink re-entry vehicle which was originally designed for the Atlas ICBM.

Beginning on January 25, 1957, the first four Thor test launches were failures. However, a number of successful test flights followed intensive studies of these early failures.

The Thor was declared operational by 1959. Operational deployment was assigned to the United Kingdom, with the first Thor delivered to RAF Feltwell in December, 1959.

A total of 20 squadrons equipped with three Thor missiles each were deployed from Yorkshire to Suffolk, England, by 1961. In the wake of significant advances in ICBM technology, Thor missiles were withdrawn from service by 1965.

Despite unbecoming inter-service rivalry and a short life as a weapons system, the Thor remains a critical vehicle in the evolution of the U.S. space program. The missile acted as the core booster for many satellite-carrying relatives, not the least of which was the Delta.

JUPITER

Classification: Intermediate-Range Ballistic Missile

Length: 60 feet, 1 inch

Diameter: 8 feet, 9 inches

Range: 1,976 miles

Date of First Cape Canaveral Launch: March 1, 1957

Date of Final Cape Canaveral Launch: January 22, 1963

Number of Cape Canaveral Launches: 36

Designed by the Army Ballistic Missile Agency (ABMA), the Jupiter missile, initially designated SM-78, represented a logical follow-up to the Redstone MRBM.

Even though research and development of the Jupiter was performed by the ABMA, the U.S. Army was never able to deploy the missile.

Late in 1955, Secretary of Defense Charles E. Wilson directed the ABMA to work in conjunction with the U.S. Navy to develop both a land-based and sea-based version of the Jupiter.

Just one year later, in his infamous "Wilson Memorandum", Wilson stunned the ABMA by stripping the U.S. Army of all missiles with a range of over 200 miles.

The U.S. Navy subsequently abandoned the Jupiter in favor of the safer, more practical solid-fueled, submarine-based Polaris missile.

The Jupiter was transferred to the U.S. Air Force. Although it eventually became the first operational U.S. IRBM, the Jupiter was never given tremendous attention by the U.S. Air Force.

The missile had competed directly with the U.S. Air Force-developed Thor IRBM. The U.S. Army-developed Jupiter had been a source of bitter rivalry between the two branches of service since its conception.

Built by Chrysler, the Jupiter first stage was powered by a Rocketdyne engine which burned liquid oxygen/ RP-1 (kerosene) liquid fuel and could produce a thrust of 150,000 pounds at liftoff.

The first stage engine's gimbaled thrust chamber was adapted directly from the canceled Navaho cruise missile. Vernier thrust and roll were controlled by the gimbaled first stage engine exhaust.

Missile guidance was provided by an ABMA-designed gyroscope and accelerometer built by Ford Instrument, Farragut and Sperry Gyroscope divisions of Sperry Rand.

An ablative technology re-entry vehicle manufactured by Goodyear shrouded a one megaton warhead, and separated from the Jupiter following the detonation of explosive bolts. A Thiokol solid-fueled motor was ignited to provide final velocity trimming.

Operational Jupiter missiles were delivered to the U.S. Air Force at a frequency of about four per month beginning in November, 1957. These could be moved during field operations inside a transporter which resembled a large steel tube.

The transporter was towed by a six-by-six truck. The missile could be raised by a hoist and held upright for long periods by an A-frame support structure.

The missile itself remained shrouded by several "petal" hinges which provided environmental protection and could be "peeled" back prior to launch operations.

Jupiter components were test flown aboard Jupiter A and Jupiter C rockets, which were not themselves Jupiters but rather modified versions of the Redstone MRBM. The first test flight of an actual Jupiter missile occurred on April 26, 1957.

In 1958, the U.S. Air Force activated the 864th and 865th Strategic Missile Squadron at the Redstone Arsenal in Huntsville, Alabama, where the Jupiter missile was designed.

Jupiter missiles were subsequently deployed by NATO troops in Italy and Turkey under U.S. supervision. The Jupiter IRBM was withdrawn from service in 1964.

Although apparently short-lived, the Jupiter program played a vital role in the history of the U.S. space program.

Development of the Jupiter missile led directly to the launch of America's first satellite aboard a Juno I rocket. The Juno I was adapted from the Redstone-based Jupiter C vehicles used to test Jupiter components.

There was also a chance that the Jupiter missile itself could have played an important role in the NASA Mercury program. In December, 1958 Mercury program managers asked ABMA to complete a feasibility analysis on how Redstone and Jupiter missiles could be modified for use in meeting Mercury test objectives.

Indeed, ABMA quickly designed specific modifications for both Redstone and Jupiter missiles that would allow the missiles to carry Mercury capsules. The Redstone design became known as the Mercury-Redstone, but it is lesser known that a Mercury-Jupiter design also emerged.

But, the vehicle never left the drawing board as NASA canceled the Mercury-Jupiter program in July, 1959. It had become clear by that time that Mercury-Redstone and Mercury-Atlas rockets would be sufficient to support Mercury test objectives.

The Jupiter missile did, however, act as the first stage for the Juno II rockets which carried a number of scientific payloads into space. Juno II, in turn, was an ancestor of the rockets which would carry men to the Moon.

And even if spurned during the NASA Mercury program, the Jupiter missile was actually able to play a role in the NASA Apollo program. Inert Jupiter missile shells ballasted with water were used as dummy upper stages for the earliest version of the Apollo-Saturn I, known as the Saturn I Block I.

BULL GOOSE

Classification: Non-Lethal Surface-Launched Cruise Missile

Length: 33 feet, 6 inches

Diameter: 2 feet

Wingspan: 24 feet, 3 inches

Range: 1,500 miles

Date of First Cape Canaveral Launch: March 13, 1957

Date of Final Cape Canaveral Launch: December 5, 1958

Number of Cape Canaveral Launches: 20

The Goose missile was not a missile in a traditional sense. The vehicle was never designed to carry an offensive weapon.

Rather, the Goose would have been used to confuse enemy defensive systems by creating a false electronic target to draw weapons away from manned bombers or actual offensive winged cruise missiles.

The vehicle was designed by Fairchild under an initial designation of SM-73. Flight development began in 1957 as XSM-73, a turbojet-powered winged cruise missile.

Originally styled as "Blue Goose" and "Bull Goose", only the latter was actually launched from Cape Canaveral.

Developmental flight test models of the Goose never actually carried passive sensors, electronic jammers or relay communications equipment as designed, primarily due to the fact that the program was canceled before these items were incorporated.

Operational Goose vehicles would have been launched from fixed shelters, assisted at launch by a Thiokol solid rocket booster and powered in flight by a turbojet which could produce 2,200 pounds of thrust.

While Goose missiles could have been launched from overseas bases for the purpose of flying over the Soviet Union, Goose bases were initially proposed for Duluth Municipal Airport, Minnesota and Ethan Allen Air Force Base, Vermont.

Launches from these bases could not possibly have supported Goose flights over the Soviet Union. This fact created a theory that Goose missiles would have been intermittently flown over the U.S. mainland to test the reliability of domestic defensive systems.

While this would have demonstrated an interesting flight scenario, the Goose was never deployed for this or any other purpose. The entire program was canceled in December, 1958.

A Bull Goose did, however, hold the distinction of being test launched from Cape Canaveral on January 31, 1958. A Juno I rocket carrying America's first satellite, Explorer I, was launched later the same day from Cape Canaveral Launch Complex 26.

POLARIS FTV

Classification: Research Rocket

Length: 40 feet, 6 inches

Finspan: 8 feet, 6 inches

Date of First Cape Canaveral Launch: April 13, 1957

Date of Final Cape Canaveral Launch: June 24, 1958

Number of Cape Canaveral Launches: 18

As Lockheed embarked on an innovative effort to develop a brand new, solid-fueled Fleet Ballistic Missile (FBM) for the U.S. Navy, a decision was made to use their existing solid-fueled X-17 research rocket as a test-bed for groundbreaking FBM technology.

A series of launches of X-17 rockets would serve to validate some of the innovations planned for incorporation on the new FBM fleet, including guidance mechanisms, nose cone technology and overall flight dynamics.

The X-17 launches would prove to save valuable time and money, since any potential technical problems could be ironed out before the actual missile prototypes were manufactured and launched.

Once the initial U.S. Navy FBM offering was named Polaris, the X-17 rockets used during flight tests became known as the Polaris Flight Test Vehicle, or Polaris FTV. In all other respects, the Polaris FTV was identical to the X-17.

ATLAS A

Classification: Inter-Continental Ballistic Missile Prototype

Length: 75 feet, 10 inches

Diameter: 10 feet

Range: 600 miles

Date of First Cape Canaveral Launch: June 11, 1957

Date of Final Cape Canaveral Launch: June 3, 1958

Number of Cape Canaveral Launches: 8

Originally developed as the first U.S. ICBM weapons system, the Atlas program rapidly evolved into an extremely viable and successful family of space boosters which remain in use today.

Atlas vehicle design can be traced back to the days following the conclusion of World War II.

In a letter issued on October 31, 1945, the U.S. Army Air Technical Service Command invited proposals from manufacturing concerns on the broad-based design of unmanned flying vehicles capable of carrying a weapons payload 20 to 5,000 miles.

Although this would have seemed preposterous several years earlier, the concept of unmanned vehicles carrying destructive weapons over great distances had been validated to the satisfaction of the U.S. military by the lethal German V-2 missile during World War II.

Consolidated Vultee Aircraft Corporation (Convair) based in San Diego, California, presented several design proposals for consideration.

On January 10, 1946, Convair was given military funding to begin preliminary design work on a class of missile capable of delivering a weapons payload 6,000 miles or greater, even surpassing the requirements originally requested.

Convair engineers first set about reviewing as many German missile documents as they could get their hands on. Both ballistic missile and more conventional jet-powered winged cruise missile concepts were explored.

By the end of 1946, Convair canceled its cruise missile efforts, perceiving that competitors had developed successful designs. Indeed, preliminary designs for Northrup's Snark and the Martin Company's Matador cruise missiles were already on the drawing board at the time.

But pioneering ballistic missile research continued at Convair, and the company received about $2 million to build ten missiles for flight testing under the MX-774 "Hiroc" (High-Altitude Rocket) designation on April 19, 1946.

Design work for the MX-774 began at Vultee Field near Downey, California in June, 1946. Originally, three distinct versions of the MX-774 were considered. The first, called MX-774 Design A and nicknamed "Teetotaler" because it did not burn alcohol, resembled a cruise missile.

MX-774 Design B, nicknamed "Old Fashioned" due to its resemblance to the V-2, was designed as a supersonic test vehicle. MX-774 Design C, nicknamed "Manhattan" due to its presumed nuclear capability, was intended to be an operational missile.

Ultimately, only the Design B version of the MX-774 was built. Fabrication of the missiles began in the fall of 1947. The first MX-774 static engine test firing was conducted on November 14, 1947.

Remarkably, this MX-774 design contained technical innovations which would actually carry through to today's Atlas vehicles, effectively laying a foundation for major breakthroughs in post-war rocketry.

These included a single-wall construction made of stainless steel rolled so thinly that the missile body had to be pressurized to keep from collapsing like a balloon.

The missile's propellants would inflate the main missile body and make it rigid, thus saving weight by eliminating the need for an internal support structure.

In the Atlas missile ultimately introduced, the skin weighed less than 2% of the fuel it carried. If the skin's thickness varied by as little as 1/1,000 of an inch, the missile's weight could increase by 100 pounds and its range could decrease by 100 miles.

The MX-774 also featured a separating nose cone which could carry scientific instrumentation or a weapons payload. This also saved critical weight since the missile body itself did not require aerodynamic equipment to guide it to a precision impact.

In addition, the missile incorporated a gimbaled engine exhaust nozzle to facilitate steering. While other ballistic missiles of the day, including the German V-2, used exhaust deflector vanes to guide the missile, gimbaled engines would set a new standard.

Giving credit where credit is due, it was Reaction Motors, Inc. and not Convair that actually developed the gimbaled engine exhaust nozzle that was adapted for use on the MX-774.

Despite this groundbreaking effort, the MX-774 project was canceled on July 1, 1947. This was just three months before the missile's first scheduled test-flight. Pentagon leadership initially felt that long-range ballistic missiles, still an unproven technology, would compete for funding with traditional manned heavy bombers.

However, the grandfather of the modern Atlas did not die. Some of the MX-774 funding remained available after official cancellation, and Convair was given permission to build and test-launch three of ten missiles originally authorized.

The first missile was completed in October, 1947. It was test-fired on a static launch stand at Convair's Ft. Loma facility on November 14, 1947. Several more static test-firings were conducted in the following months.

Static engine tests were completed by May, 1948. The first MX-774 was then trucked to the White Sands Missile Range in New Mexico for flight testing. It was erected at an old, modified V-2 launch platform.

Indeed, the MX-774 was described as a "streamlined" version of the German V-2. The missile was 31 feet, 7 inches long by 2 feet, 6 inches wide and had a finspan of about 6 feet. It weighed 1,200 pounds empty.

The first MX-774 static engine firing on the launch platform was conducted on May 26, 1948. Several more static test-firings followed. The first MX-774 was launched on July 13, 1948. The missile's propulsion system shut down unexpectedly about one minute into the flight, causing it to crash prematurely.

Much of the wreckage was recovered and examined, and it was concluded that a major flaw in missile hardware probably did not cause the engine cutoff.

The second MX-774 was launched on September 27, 1948. It flew to a height of 40 miles before breaking up due to an undetermined malfunction. However, flight dynamics were verified, and useable data was transmitted from the missile to the ground during the test.

The third and last MX-774 was launched on December 2, 1948. A mysterious propulsion system cutoff similar to that experienced in the first test-flight occurred, although the missile reached a higher altitude before dropping to the ground.

Convair continued ballistic missile research and design work following the expiration of the MX-774 project. At the time, U.S. Air Force funding centered around more conventional winged cruise missile applications, most notably the Navajo, built by North American.

Regardless of this funding situation, Convair conceived another pioneering mainstay of the eventual Atlas missile in 1949. This was the "one and one-half stage" propulsion system.

In this configuration, a series of "booster" and "sustainer" engines would all be ignited at liftoff. During the flight, the booster engines would shut down, then be jettisoned along with their associated fairing structure.

The sustainer engines would remain burning after jettison of the booster engines, remaining attached to the vehicle for the duration of its flight.

While a debate still rages as to whether or not a configuration whereby all engines are ignited at liftoff can truly be defined as more than one stage, the "one and one-half stage" description has stuck with Atlas vehicles ever since.

It was also in 1949 that the U.S. military showed a renewed interest in ballistic missile technology. In August of that year, the Soviet Union exploded their first atomic weapon.

The start of the Korean War on June 25, 1950 indicated yet another need to press ahead with long-range missile development. On January 23, 1951, Convair was granted a contract under what was called the MX-1593 project.

The U.S. Air Force sought to determine the most effective method of delivering nuclear weapons over vast distances. Again, winged cruise missiles were pitted against ballistic missiles, although both would eventually be approved.

When the MX-1593 contract was issued, Convair already had available for the U.S. Air Force detailed ballistic missile design proposals that had been refined in-house following the expiration of the MX-774. The company offered design proposals for both pure ballistic and semi-ballistic concepts.

In the pure ballistic approach, the missile would fly a ballistic pattern to its target. In the semi-ballistic approach, the missile would be launched in a ballistic pattern, but would glide toward its target using wings.

A firm decision was made by the U.S. Air Force to press ahead with Convair's pure ballistic missile warhead delivery system in September, 1951. It was decided that the semi-ballistic version would be too easy to intercept. Even though a pure ballistic guidance system had yet to be developed, the semi-ballistic approach was scrapped.

The MX-1593 stage of Atlas development is worthy of special note because the name of the long-lived missile and rocket program was approved at that time. In January, 1951, Convair engineer Karel J. Bossart proposed the name "Atlas" for the company's missile.

It was perhaps a bit optimistic at the time to assume that an "Atlas" missile fleet would "carry the world on its shoulders" like its Greek god namesake.

It was somewhat more apparent that the "Atlas Corporation" was the parent company of Convair, and perhaps deserved special tribute. Other names considered by Convair included "Boxcar" and "Hot Rod".

The U.S. Air Force approved the name "Atlas" for the Convair missile program in August, 1951, although a few more changes in numerical designations were in store.

The "Atlas Missile" was briefly reclassified as the "Atlas Bomber" and designated B-65 late in 1951. Early in 1952, the "Atlas Bomber" was reclassified as the "Atlas Missile" and designated SM-65.

In July, 1952, the U.S. Air Force allocated additional funds to the Atlas program. After a progress review in December of the same year, a decision was made to continue development of the missile.

Soon afterward, the U.S. Air Force gave the Atlas its highest priority rating of "1A" and went forward on what is best described as a "crash course" development program. The new U.S. rush to develop an operational ICBM was primarily due to the "cold war" combined with scientific advances of the day.

In 1953, the U.S. Atomic Energy Commission produced a classified report indicating that nuclear weapons would soon be produced that could be light and small enough to carry aboard an ICBM.

It was also apparent that the Soviet Union was well underway with its own missile programs, which combined Soviet research with captured German V-2 technology. U.S. missile programs, including Atlas, were accelerated due to this very tangible military threat.

Convair recommended that Atlas test missiles similar to the proposed operational ICBM be produced to validate the missile's airframe, launch systems and propulsion hardware. Any potential problems with the basic missile design could be ironed out in this test phase.

Convair and the U.S. Air Force determined that the fabrication of test missiles which closely resembled an operational model could quicken the development of an operational weapons system by as much as a year.

The risk of uncovering a major flaw which might scuttle the entire Atlas program was outweighed by the time savings leading to ultimate deployment of the missile.

Therefore, U.S. Air Force approval was given to Convair for the development of two series of Atlas test missiles in May, 1953. The first Atlas test series was designated X-11, while the second, more advanced test series, was designated X-12.

By 1954, Solar Aircraft Company completed the first Atlas thin-skin tank. In August of the same year, the missile's design was modified to accommodate practical improvements in nuclear warhead design.

In October, 1954, a decision was made to make the most significant Atlas modification to date. This was a reduction from a planned five engines to three. Since nuclear weapons payloads had become smaller and lighter, less overall thrust would be needed to carry them.

The five-engine Atlas would have been 90 feet long and 12 feet wide, while the first three-engine Atlas actually introduced was scaled down to 75 feet, 10 inches long and 10 feet wide.

The Atlas missile design was frozen in December, 1954. On December 16, 1954 Convair and the U.S. Air Force made the first official public announcement that Atlas production was underway. Atlas was intended to be revealed by its code name "Model 7" but in fact the name Atlas had appeared in Aviation Week magazine as early as March 8, 1954.

After an intensive series of inspections of Atlas production designs, the U.S. Air Force officially issued to Convair a contract for the long-term continuation of the Atlas program on January 14, 1955.

The Atlas was given its final numerical designation of Weapons System-107A (WS-107A), calling for a missile capable of carrying a nuclear payload 6,000 to 9,000 miles with a circular error of not more than ten miles.

It should be noted that some sources exclusively refer to the Atlas weapons system as WS-107A-1. This is primarily due to the fact that the Titan missile program was later designated WS-107A-2.

Since the Titan was designed well after Atlas development was already underway, the initial designation of WS-107A alone is historically accurate for the Atlas missile.

However, it is equally acceptable to refer to the Atlas program as WS-107A-1 for the specific purpose of contrasting it with the Titan designation of WS-107A-2. Strictly speaking, both missiles were initiated under WS-107A, with Atlas being first and Titan second.

Upon receiving the WS-107A production contract, Convair subsequently began construction of a new facility called Convair Astronautics based in Kearney Mesa, outside San Diego, California.

In May of 1955, the U.S. Air Force inspected a mock-up of the Atlas missile, and about three months later gave their final approval for the construction of the first operational test vehicles.

The first Atlas missile was completed in August, 1956, although this missile was not built for flight. It was delivered to the U.S. Air Force for static systems testing at Sycamore Canyon, California on August 29, 1956.

The first Atlas to arrive at Cape Canaveral was a dummy version designed to test compatibility of the Atlas body with launch systems. At the time, Atlas missiles were too large to transport by aircraft. Instead, the missile had to be transported aboard a specially designed truck trailer.

The Atlas "cradle" which delivered the missile from the factory to the launch pad was built by Goodyear Aircraft Corporation. It was 64 feet long by 14 feet wide and required two "back-seat" drivers to maneuver the vehicle around turns. The dummy Atlas left San Diego aboard such a trailer on October 1, 1956.

The trip was arduous, at best. Due to the size of the trailer, tight turns and all bridges and underpasses under 13 feet, 10 inches high were avoided. To maintain security, detours were made around large cities and a police escort was employed.

The journey was made in daylight hours only, and resulted in numerous pit and overnight stops. The missile body itself was shrouded in an aluminum-colored canvas. During this maiden trip, security officials were reportedly dismayed during a pit stop when a child identified the "secret" cargo as an Atlas missile.

The first Atlas completed its 2,622-mile journey to the Cape in nine days. A flight-ready Atlas would soon be able to cover the equivalent distance in about 18 minutes.

The first flight-ready Atlas, designated Atlas #4A, was received at Cape Canaveral in December, 1956. The foundation was thus laid for a plethora of Atlas missile and rocket launches which followed.

Originating as the X-11, Atlas A was the name given to the first series of Atlas missiles delivered to Cape Canaveral for flight testing.

Atlas A missiles were designed primarily to test the airframe and propulsion system, which could be accomplished in relatively short-range flights. For this reason, the Atlas A did not employ a sustainer engine.

Thus, it was the only "single stage" version of the Atlas. It was, however, an improved version of the X-11 as conceived. The X-11 was originally designed to fly with just one booster engine.

The Atlas A operated with two North American booster engines, each of which provided a thrust of 120,000 pounds at liftoff. It also employed two vernier engines, located on opposite sides of the missile above the booster engine fairing.

The vernier engines, a trademark of Atlas vehicles, were designed to control the roll of the missile and trim its final flight velocity.

The booster and vernier engines were all fed by liquid oxygen/RP-1 (kerosene) liquid propellant, and all engines were ignited at liftoff.

The missile carried a semi-inertial guidance system which was supported by radio commands from ground stations.

In general terms, the Atlas A made a pre-programmed turn to a ballistic trajectory at an altitude of about 20,000 feet. The two booster engines shut down about two and one-half minutes into the flight.

In a flight profile unique to the Atlas A, the two booster engines did not need to be jettisoned after shutdown, and remained attached to the missile's main body to water impact.

About ten seconds following booster engine shutdown, the two vernier engines shut down, and the nose cone separated. By this time, the nose cone had been guided to its proper flight path, and could reach its target without further guidance.

On June 11, 1957 an Atlas A had the distinction of becoming the first Atlas launched from Cape Canaveral. The missile strayed off course and was destroyed by the Range Safety Officer less than one minute into its flight. However, some test objectives regarding the missile's launch systems and airframe were met.

Although only three of the eight Atlas A missiles launched from Cape Canaveral completed their flights as planned, the "failures" were themselves instrumental in determining that the Atlas airframe was strong enough to survive violent twists, turns and loops in low-altitude "heavy air".

The A Series Tests also determined that the Atlas launch system and gimbaled engine flight control system worked effectively.

JUNO I

Classification: Space Launch Vehicle

Length: 68 feet, 7 inches

Diameter: 5 feet, 10 inches

Finspan: 13 feet

Date of First Cape Canaveral Launch: January 31, 1958

Date of Final Cape Canaveral Launch: October 22, 1958

Number of Cape Canaveral Launches: 6

Arguably one of the most significant space launch vehicles in the history of the U.S. space program, the Juno I was a modified Redstone MRBM designed specifically to carry lightweight payloads into low-Earth orbit.

Although the Juno I was nearly identical to the Jupiter C research rocket from which it was adapted, the names Juno I and Jupiter C should not be interchanged, as is frequently the case.

The Jupiter C, or Jupiter "Composite", was used exclusively to perform re-entry tests of Jupiter IRBM nosec-one technology. In this configuration, a powered fourth stage was not flown. Technically speaking, this made the Jupiter C a three-stage rocket.

On the Juno I, an operational fourth stage was flown which remained attached to the satellite payload. Thus, Juno I is a name used to distinguish a vehicle used specifically to launch satellites.

Jupiter C had concluded its role in Jupiter component testing prior to the vehicle's modification to satellite launcher. As a result, Jupiter C was officially renamed Juno at the request of Dr. William Pickering, head of the Jet Propulsion Laboratory, on November 18, 1957.

In addition to distinguishing the rocket as a satellite launcher, the name Juno also served to divert attention away from the Jupiter IRBM program for which the Jupiter C was originally designed. The name Juno was later changed to Juno I to distinguish it from the Juno II.

The Juno I was powered at liftoff by a single Rocketdyne engine capable of producing a thrust of 83,000 pounds. The engine burned liquid oxygen and Hydyne liquid fuel.

Hydyne liquid fuel, a combination of 60% unsymmetrical dimethyl hydrazine (UDMH) and 40% diethylene-triamine, replaced alcohol previously used to power the Redstone first stage. This increased the first stage thrust by 8,000 pounds over the Jupiter C.

The Juno I second stage was a cluster of 11 Thiokol Baby Sergeant solid-fuel motors which produced a combined thrust of 16,500 pounds. The Juno I third stage was a cluster of three Thiokol Baby Sergeant solid-fuel motors producing a combined thrust of 5,400 pounds.

One Thiokol Baby Sergeant solid-fuel motor, permanently attached to the satellite payload, made up the Juno I fourth stage. The fourth stage motor provided 1,800 pounds of thrust and accompanied the satellite payload into orbit.

Each Baby Sergeant solid-fueled motor was 46 inches long by 6 inches wide. Each of the second and third stage Baby Sergeant motors burned 50 pounds of T17-E2 solid fuel. The fourth stage Baby Sergeant motor burned 50 pounds of JPL-532A solid fuel, a slightly more efficient fuel than that burned in the second and third stages.

A distinctive rotating "tub" covered the clustered second and third stages, and was quite visible during liftoff and flight. It provided balance and stability to these stages during ascent.

Following launch, the first stage engine burned for about 155 seconds. After first stage burnout and separation, the clustered upper stages were allowed to coast to their highest altitude. Once the highest altitude was achieved, the upper stages were sequentially fired.

The second stage was fired for about six seconds, followed by a two second pause to allow separation. The third stage was then fired for about six seconds, followed by a two second pause to allow separation. Finally, the fourth stage was fired for about six seconds to carry the attached satellite payload into orbit. Payloads carried by the Juno I typically weighed about 30 pounds.

Following scrubs on January 29 and January 30, a Juno I bearing the letters "UE" (Redstone #29; see Jupiter C) successfully launched Explorer I, the first U.S. satellite. The Juno I was launched from Cape Canaveral Launch Pad 26A at 10:48 p.m. EST on January 31, 1958.

This was followed by five more Juno I satellite launch attempts. A Juno I bearing the letters "UV" (Redstone #26) was launched from Cape Canaveral Launch Pad 26A on March 5, 1958. The fourth stage failed to fire in this unsuccessful attempt to launch Explorer II.

A Juno I bearing the letters "UT" (Redstone #24) was launched from Cape Canaveral Launch Pad 5 on March 26, 1958. This Juno I successfully carried Explorer III into orbit. A Juno I bearing the letters "TT" (Redstone #44) launched from Cape Canaveral Launch Pad 5 on July 26, 1958 successfully carried Explorer IV into orbit.

The last two Juno I launches were failures. A Juno I bearing the letters "TI" (Redstone #47) launched from Cape Canaveral Launch Pad 5 on August 24, 1958 failed to carry Explorer V into orbit when the Redstone booster bumped the upper stages, sending them out of control.

Finally, a Juno I bearing the letters "HE" (Redstone #49 should have been lettered "TE" according to code, but "HE" was used instead) was launched from Cape Canaveral Launch Pad 5 on October 22, 1958. The upper stage clusters broke off in an unsuccessful attempt to deploy the Beacon I balloon-type satellite.

THOR-ABLE 0

Classification: Research Rocket/Space Launch Vehicle

Length: 90 feet

Diameter: 8 feet

Date of First Cape Canaveral Launch: April 23, 1958

Date of Final Cape Canaveral Launch: July 23, 1958

Number of Cape Canaveral Launches: 3

Using the Thor IRBM as a core booster, the Thor-Able 0 rocket was introduced in 1958. The vehicle was originally designed to support high-altitude U.S. Air Force and civilian re-entry vehicle research.

The Thor-Able 0 was later modified to carry small satellites into orbit, and became the first Thor-based variant to do so. Thor-Able 0 was the first generation of what would become the Delta family of space launch vehicles which remain in use today.

The Thor-Able 0 employed a Rocketdyne first stage engine which burned liquid oxygen/RP-1 (kerosene) liquid fuel and could produce 150,000 pounds of thrust at launch.

The second and third stages were adapted directly from the Vanguard rocket. An Aerojet second stage engine burned IRFNA/UDMH solid fuel and could produce a 7,575-pound thrust.

An Altair solid-fueled third stage engine could produce a thrust of 2,760 pounds.

The first three Thor-Able 0 rockets were launched from Cape Canaveral in support of the Atlas missile research and development program. These Thor-Able 0 rockets were powerful enough to duplicate the intended Atlas full-range flight distance of 6,000 miles.

For this reason, Thor-Able 0 rockets were selected to produce high speed re-entry data of the ablative-type heat resistant material proposed for Atlas missile nosecones.

But in addition to supporting the tests of vital Atlas missile hardware, these Thor-Able 0 flights also carried out some groundbreaking biological research. Each of the three nose cones launched in this test series carried a lone mouse as passenger.

Electronic monitoring of these mice would determine whether or not animals could survive a long-range missile flight. These tests would prove to be significant since the mice would reach maximum altitudes of 600 to 1,000 miles above Earth during their journey, and experience long periods of weightlessness and gravity stress.

These Thor-Able 0 flights did provide useful data on ablative nose cone technology, but the mice did not fare so well. The first of these Thor-Able 0 rockets carried a mouse named "Mouse-In-Able-1" (MIA-1), nicknamed "Minnie Mouse" and was launched on April 23, 1958. The rocket exploded due to a first stage gearbox failure.

The second of these Thor-Able 0 rockets carried a mouse named "Mouse-In-Able-2" (MIA-2) and was launched on July 9, 1958. The mouse survived its entire flight, but recovery crews were not able to locate the nose cone.

The last Thor-Able mouse, named "Wickie Mouse" in honor of the nickname of Cape Canaveral journalist Mercer "Wickie" Livermore, was launched on July 23, 1958. This mouse also survived its flight, but recovery crews were not able to locate the nose cone.

Even though the nosecones were not recovered in the two successful Thor-Able 0 research flights, the fact that flights of 6,000 miles were achieved prompted Douglas Aircraft to propose an ICBM version of the Thor called Thor-Intercontinental, or "Thoric".

Proposals for a Thoric missile were quickly rejected by the U.S. Air Force, however, since development of the Atlas and Titan ICBM weapons systems were already well underway.

Thor-Able 0 research rockets were, however, modified to carry out satellite launching missions. Each Thor-Able 0 was capable of carrying a maximum 300-pound payload into low-Earth orbit.

BOLD ORION

Classification: Air-Launched Ballistic Missile Prototype

Length: 37 feet

Range: 1,100 miles

Date of First Cape Canaveral Launch: May 26, 1958

Date of Final Cape Canaveral Launch: October 13, 1959

Number of Cape Canaveral Launches: 12

Bold Orion was a research and development program of the Martin Company, Baltimore (later Martin Marietta). In 1958, the company was offered a short-term contract with the U.S. Air Force to determine if air-launched ballistic missiles (ALBM) were feasible.

An ALBM would differ dramatically from cruise missiles already under development at the time. Cruise missiles flew toward their targets somewhat like traditional aircraft. An ALBM, however, could be dropped from an aircraft, then fly a ballistic path into space on the way to its target.

Although a number of ground-launched ballistic missiles were already being vigorously developed by 1958, Bold Orion represented the first ballistic missile that could be launched from the air.

Designated ALBM-199B, the Bold Orion program introduced a series of test missiles which were launched over Atlantic Missile Range waters from B-47 aircraft.

Since the Bold Orion program was highly secret in nature and very short-lived, specific records regarding the vehicles themselves have not survived. However, certain anecdotal accounts have shed some small light on the program.

Actual vehicles flown in the course of the Bold Orion program were fashioned by combining elements of existing missile programs, so at first the test vehicles may have differed from one to the next.

After several early versions of the Bold Orion did not perform well in flight tests, Martin engineers apparently adapted Sergeant missile components as a first stage and Vanguard rocket third stage components as a second stage.

The result was a very effective two-stage, solid-fueled missile that is reported to have flown a maximum distance of 1,100 miles and successfully demonstrated that ALBM weapons were feasible.

According to U.S. Air Force records, a total of 12 Bold Orion missiles were launched from B-47 aircraft over Atlantic Missile Range waters between May 26, 1958 and October 13, 1959.

The last of these launches was extremely significant. The Bold Orion launched from a B-47 aircraft flying at an altitude of 35,000 feet on October 13, 1959 was guided on a ballistic path 1,000 miles north, into the area near Wallops Island, Virginia.

As this Bold Orion flew, the Explorer VI satellite, traveling at a speed of about 18,000 m.p.h., approached its closest point to Earth at an altitude of 156 miles. The Bold Orion was aimed at a point about ten miles ahead of Explorer VI at approximately the same altitude.

Radar systems continuously tracked the missile as it flew. In addition, the Bold Orion transmitted radio signals to ground stations and intermittently released pyrotechnic flares that aided in visual tracking.

A combination of these tracking methods determined that the Bold Orion missile passed within four miles of the Explorer VI satellite, a remarkable achievement in its day.

Thus, the Bold Orion program was not only the first to demonstrate that ALBM weapons systems were feasible, it also was the first to demonstrate that the interception of satellites by ballistic missile weapons was possible.

ATLAS B

Classification: Inter-Continental Ballistic Missile Prototype

Length: 75 feet, 10 inches

Diameter: 10 feet

Range: 6,000 miles

Date of First Cape Canaveral Launch: July 19, 1958

Date of Final Cape Canaveral Launch: February 14, 1959

Number of Cape Canaveral Launches: 9

Originating as the X-12, Atlas B was the name given to the second series of Atlas missiles delivered to Cape Canaveral for flight testing.

Since the Atlas B missile was built to test booster and nose cone separation as well as the overall propulsion system, longer-range flights were needed. This required the Atlas B to employ an operating one and one-half stage booster/sustainer engine combination.

In order for a B Series Test to be considered completely successful, five events called "Marks" needed to be completed. Mark One was booster engine shutdown, Mark Two was booster engine separation, Mark Three was sustainer engine cutoff, Mark Four was vernier engine cutoff and Mark Five was nose cone separation.

To do this, the Atlas B needed to fly nearly ten times farther than the Atlas A.

The Atlas B employed two North American booster engines and one North American sustainer engine. The sustainer engine was located in between the two booster engines. The engines each had a thrust of 120,000 pounds at liftoff.

Like the Atlas A, the missile used two vernier engines to control roll and trim final velocity. All engines were fed by liquid oxygen/RP-1 (kerosene) liquid propellant.

Like the Atlas A, the Atlas B carried a semi-inertial guidance system supported by radio commands from ground stations.

All engines ignited at liftoff. At an altitude of about 16,000 feet, the Atlas B performed a pre-programmed turn to a ballistic trajectory.

About two minutes into the flight, the two booster engines shut down and were jettisoned. The sustainer engine remained firing for about an additional two minutes, staying attached to the missile body to its final water impact.

Following sustainer engine cutoff, the two vernier engines remained firing for about 30 seconds. Following cutoff of the vernier engines, the nose cone separated, continuing on toward its target without further guidance.

An Atlas B was first launched from Cape Canaveral on July 19, 1958. The missile lost thrust about 43 seconds into the flight, exploded and fell into the Atlantic Ocean about three miles downrange.

In stark contrast, an Atlas B launched from Cape Canaveral successfully completed the first full-range Atlas test flight on November 28, 1958. The missile ended its flight about 6,000 miles downrange of the launch site.

JASON

Classification: Research Rocket

Length: 57 Feet

Diameter: 23 Inches

Date of First Cape Canaveral Launch: August 14, 1958

Date of Final Cape Canaveral Launch: September 2, 1958

Number of Cape Canaveral Launches: 6

Jason was a 5-stage solid-fueled rocket. It was comprised of an Honest John first stage, a Nike second stage, a Nike third stage, a Recruit fourth stage and a T-55 fifth stage. The rocket weighed 7,340 pounds and could produce a liftoff thrust of 82,100 pounds. Used in suborbital applications only, the Jason rocket was capable of carrying a 125-pound payload to a maximum altitude of 500 miles.

All of the Jason launches from Cape Canaveral were in support of Project Argus, a series of high altitude nuclear detonations. Jason rockets carried a payload which could measure levels of radiation trapped in the upper atmosphere as a result of these detonations.

THOR-ABLE I

Classification: Space Launch Vehicle

Length: 90 feet

Diameter: 8 feet

Date of First Cape Canaveral Launch: August 17, 1958

Date of Final Cape Canaveral Launch: November 8, 1958

Number of Cape Canaveral Launches: 3

Thor-Able I was the name given to a close relative of the Thor-Able 0. In fact, the first three stages of the Thor-Able I were identical to those of the Thor-Able 0.

Essentially a Thor-Able 0 with an added fourth stage, the Thor-Able I was designed specifically to carry Pioneer spacecraft toward the Moon.

The solid-propellant fourth stage motor remained attached to the payload. In this application, the third stage was spin-stabilized at 120 r.p.m.

The Thor-Able I could carry a maximum 84-pound payload to a lunar trajectory.

ALBM 199-C

Classification: Air-Launched Ballistic Missile Prototype

Date of First Cape Canaveral Launch: September 5, 1958

Date of Final Cape Canaveral Launch: June 4, 1959

Number of Cape Canaveral Launches: 3

Like the Martin Company Bold Orion (designated ALBM 199-B) ALBM 199-C represented a short-term research and development program funded by the Air Force in the late 1950's to determine the feasibility of launching ballistic missiles from aircraft. ALBM 199-C was a joint venture of Convair and Lockheed.

Precious little is known about the ALBM 199-C, which apparently never received a name. Since it was designed to be launched from B-58 Hustler aircraft, the missile has been referred to in anecdotal accounts as the "B-58 ALBM" (pronounced B-58 AL-BUM).

Just three ALBM 199-C missiles were launched between September 5, 1958 and June 4, 1959. Each was launched from a B-58 Hustler, which carried one missile slung under the center of the aircraft. The B-58 Hustler flights originated at Eglin Air Force Base, Florida and the missiles were launched over Atlantic waters east of Cape Canaveral.

Aside from a few photos and anecdotal accounts, information about the ALBM 199-C vehicle and its performance are scarce. This is likely due to the limited number of launches, the classified nature of the program and the fact that an identifiable weapons program never emerged.

POLARIS A1

Classification: Fleet Ballistic Missile

Note: Fleet Ballistic Missiles are also referred to as Submarine-Launched Ballistic Missiles

Length: 28 feet

Diameter: 4 feet, 6 inches

Range: 1,380 miles

Date of First Cape Canaveral Launch: September 24, 1958

Date of Final Cape Canaveral Launch: September 4, 1963

Number of Cape Canaveral Launches: 109

Developed in the late 1950's, the Polaris family provided the U.S. with its first submarine-based nuclear missiles. The first generation Polaris A1 became the ancestor of a missile family which comprises the backbone of current U.S. nuclear offensive capability.

In 1955, the U.S. Navy was directed to participate in a joint venture with the Army Ballistic Missile Agency (ABMA) to create a sea-based version of the Jupiter IRBM.

During the course of Jupiter testing, it became clear that the missile's liquid fuels, especially volatile liquid oxygen, provided an unacceptable hazard during at-sea operations.

It was also recognized that the Jupiter, or any similar liquid-fueled missile, was too difficult to maintain and operate either aboard ship or submarine.

For these reasons, the U.S. Navy abandoned the Jupiter program in December, 1956. Instead, the option of deploying a solid-fueled missile was vigorously explored.

The need for a sea-based missile using solid fuel, lightweight construction, miniature inertial guidance, small nuclear devices and cold gas ejection from submarine tubes during uncertain environmental conditions provided considerable engineering challenges.

With the highest military priority, Lockheed was assigned the task of developing this ambitious missile program. Lockheed selected Polyurethane Ammonium Perchlorate (PU/AP) solid fuel for the two-stage vehicle to eliminate the hazards associated with liquid fuel.

In addition, a procedure for gas-propelled launching from submarine tubes was developed to eliminate the hazard of firing the missile's first stage aboard ship.

Test versions of the missile were first known as AX-6, then A1-X, but the name Polaris A1 was ultimately selected along with the military numerical designation of UGM-27A.

Aerojet-General first and second stage engines were encased in a steel frame. The first stage engine had four rotary exhaust nozzles, while the second stage engine had one. Each missile could carry a 500 kiloton nuclear warhead.

The missile's MIT/GE/Hughes inertial guidance system was linked to a GE fire control. A Westinghouse/MIT launch control system activated the high pressure gas flow which forced the missile out of its launch tube.

The Polaris A1 was suitable for launching from ships as well as submarines and the U.S.S. Observation Island was outfitted for Polaris A1 launches with 2 missile tubes.

The U.S. Navy also ordered a total of 41 Fleet Ballistic Missile (FBM) submarines, with five to be modified from existing submarines and 36 to be built from scratch.

The first five FBM submarines were ingeniously created by simply splitting existing submarines in two and inserting a 130-foot section amidship to house 16 missile tubes and support facilities.

The first of these, named SSN 589 Scorpion, was renamed SSBN 598 George Washington following its completion to FBM status. Since it was the first FBM submarine completed, all five of these renovated submarines became known as the George Washington Class.

SSBN 598 George Washington supported the first U.S. submarine-based missile launches. On July 20, 1960 a total of two Polaris A1 missiles were launched from the submarine as it sat submerged just off the coast of Cape Canaveral.

Carrying 16 Polaris A1 missiles, SSBN 598 George Washington became the first operational FBM on November 15, 1960. But only the five George Washington Class submarines were actually deployed with Polaris A1 missiles.

By this time, the upgraded Polaris A2 was already under development. As a result, the first five built-from-scratch FBM submarines, beginning with SSBN 608 Ethan Allen, and thus called the Ethan Allen Class, carried Polaris A1 missiles for test launches only.

The Polaris A1 was officially retired from service on October 14, 1965 when the last George Washington Class submarine, SSBN 602 Abraham Lincoln, returned to port.

JUNO II

Classification: Space Launch Vehicle

Length: 76 feet, 7 inches

Diameter: 8 feet, 9 inches

Date of First Cape Canaveral Launch: December 6, 1958

Date of Final Cape Canaveral Launch: May 24, 1961

Number of Cape Canaveral Launches: 10

A marriage of the Jupiter IRBM as first stage and Juno I upper stages, the Juno II was able to carry a 100-pound payload to low-Earth orbit.

A Rocketdyne first stage engine burned liquid oxygen/RP-1 (kerosene) liquid fuel and could produce a thrust of 150,000 pounds at liftoff.

The second, third and fourth stage configuration was identical to that of the Juno I.

Like the Juno I, the heavily clustered second and third stages were covered by a rotating "tub" to provide balance and stability. This "tub" was not visible on the Juno II, however, since an outer fairing was incorporated to improve aerodynamics and safety.

The Juno name was also applied to the next generation of space launch vehicles designed by the Army Ballistic Missile Agency (ABMA), including a proposed Juno V super booster. The Juno program was eventually transferred to NASA and renamed Saturn.

In a very real sense, the pioneering work of the ABMA, culminating in the successful use of Juno I and Juno II space launch vehicles, led directly to the development of the rockets which would carry men to the Moon.

ATLAS-SCORE

Classification: Space Launch Vehicle

Length: 85 feet

Diameter: 10 feet

Date of First Cape Canaveral Launch: December 18, 1958

Date of Final Cape Canaveral Launch: December 18, 1958

Number of Cape Canaveral Launches: 1

Atlas-Score was an Atlas B test missile with a nose cone modified to carry the Score active communications experiment into low-Earth orbit.

An Atlas-Score successfully carried the 8,750-pound Score payload, nicknamed "Chatterbox", into orbit on December 18, 1958.

With the exception of the jettisoned booster engines, the entire Atlas missile body accompanied the payload into orbit.

Since the payload never separated, in effect the Atlas-Score itself became a satellite. The Score payload included an audio tape machine which broadcast President Eisenhower's pre-recorded 58-word Christmas message to the world.

58

ATLAS C

Classification: Inter-Continental Ballistic Missile Prototype

Length: 82 feet, 6 inches

Diameter: 10 feet

Range: 6,000 miles

Date of First Cape Canaveral Launch: December 23, 1958

Date of Final Cape Canaveral Launch: August 24, 1959

Number of Cape Canaveral Launches: 6

Designed for long-range guidance and nose cone tests, the Atlas C was configured very closely to what would become the operational Atlas ICBM.

It incorporated an improved booster/sustainer engine configuration and carried a recoverable nose cone data capsule, which carried instrumentation that recorded valuable in-flight test data.

The Atlas C carried two Rocketdyne booster engines, each with a thrust of 165,000 pounds. A single Rocketdyne sustainer engine produced a thrust of 57,000 pounds while two Rocketdyne vernier engines produced a thrust of 1,000 pounds each.

All of the engines were fed by liquid oxygen/RP-1 (kerosene) liquid propellant, and all engines were ignited at liftoff.

Like its predecessors, the Atlas C used a semi-inertial guidance system supported by radio commands from ground stations.

Considered a semi-operational training and test vehicle, an Atlas C was first launched from Cape Canaveral on December 23, 1958. The missile's flight data capsule was not recovered, but all other test objectives were met.

An Atlas C carried the first recoverable ablative technology nose cone. During the last Atlas C test on August 24, 1959, the missile's nose cone was recovered following a successful 6,000-mile, full-range flight.

THOR-ABLE II

Classification: Research Rocket

Length: 90 feet

Diameter: 8 feet

Date of First Cape Canaveral Launch: January 23, 1959

Date of Final Cape Canaveral Launch: April 1, 1960

Number of Cape Canaveral Launches: 8

Identical to the Thor-Able, Thor-Able II was simply the name given to the version of the Thor-Able which was used for high-altitude re-entry vehicle testing. The vehicle was not used to launch satellites.

The name distinguished the Thor-Able II from its satellite-bearing relative, Thor-Able I.

TITAN I

Classification: Inter-Continental Ballistic Missile

Length: 98 feet

Diameter: 10 feet

Range: 8,000 miles

Date of First Cape Canaveral Launch: February 6, 1959

Date of Final Cape Canaveral Launch: January 29, 1962

Number of Cape Canaveral Launches: 47

Under Weapons System 107A-2 (WS-107A-2), a development contract for an ICBM surpassing the capabilities of the Atlas was granted to the Martin Company (later Martin Marietta) in October, 1955. The company subsequently built a virgin production facility in Denver, Colorado.

The missile received an initial designation of SM-68. The name "Titan" after the Greek mythological father of Zeus was recommended for SM-68 by Martin Company public relations man Joe Rowland.

A pre-production version of the Titan ICBM was called Titan J, while a version designed to be compatible with launch facilities at Vandenberg Air Force Base, California, became known as Titan V (the letter "V" as opposed to the Roman Numeral "V").

Of course, the version of the missile which was ultimately deployed by the U.S. Air Force carried the name Titan I.

Inertial guidance originally intended for use on the Titan I was transferred to the Atlas program. Instead, a redesigned radio controlled guidance system from Western Electric, Sperry and Remington Rand Univac was employed.

Remington Rand Univac built groundbreaking digital technology computer components for the Titan I guidance system.

First stage propulsion for the Titan I was provided by an Aerojet engine with twin-gimbaled chambers each capable of providing 150,000 pounds of thrust at launch. The first stage engine was fed by liquid oxygen/RP-1 (kerosene) liquid fuel.

The first test launch of a Titan I occurred on February 6, 1959. For this flight, only an operational first stage was employed. A dummy second stage was ballasted with water.

The Titan I second stage was powered by an Aerojet engine which could produce an 80,000-pound thrust. Like the first stage, the Titan I second stage burned liquid oxygen/RP-1 (kerosene) liquid fuel.

The total vehicle could carry a four-megaton warhead which was housed inside an Avco re-entry vehicle.

Operational launch complexes for the Titan I may best be described as huge underground cities. Underground areas were enormously enlarged and included sophisticated radar guidance and power stations. Reaction time to launch a Titan I was about 20 minutes.

Rapid propellant loading systems and a high-speed hoist were employed. Although the Titan I was designed to be lifted out of its silo prior to launch, a test launch from Vandenberg Air Force Base, California on May 3, 1961 demonstrated that in-silo launches were possible.

The Titan I became operational at Lowry Air Force Base, Colorado on April 18, 1962. With a numerical designation of HGM-25A, Titan I deployment was completed in early 1963.

A total of six Strategic Air Command (SAC) Titan I squadrons were activated. Each squadron supported nine missiles, providing SAC with a total fleet of 54.

Two Titan I squadrons were deployed at Lowry Air Force Base, Colorado. The remaining four Titan I squadrons were located at Beale Air Force Base, California, Mountain Home Air Force Base, Idaho, Ellsworth Air Force Base, South Dakota and Larson Air Force Base, Washington.

The Titan I fleet was deactivated by 1966 in the wake of improved ICBM technology. The Titan I was never modified for space flight.

ALPHA DRACO

Classification: Research Rocket

Length: 46 feet, 1 inch

Diameter: 2 feet, 7 inches

Finspan: 7 feet, 1 inch

Date of First Cape Canaveral Launch: February 16, 1959

Date of Final Cape Canaveral Launch: April 27, 1959

Number of Cape Canaveral Launches: 3

Alpha Draco, also known as Model 122B Test Vehicle, was built by McDonnell Aircraft in support of Air Force high-altitude research activities. Just three were launched from Cape Canaveral.

Launched from a mobile trailer/erector launcher designed for the Honest John missile, Alpha Draco was a two-stage solid-fueled rocket. It carried an aeroballistic nosecone payload.

Although the rocket was launched like a ballistic missile weapon, the payload was designed to reach a high altitude, then be placed on a level flight path by utilizing its own lifting characteristics, which could be done without the use of wings.

Since the payload could then glide toward its target unpowered, without reaching space altitudes, a weapon utilizing this capability could theoretically carry a heavier weapons payload than a purely ballistic missile weapon. It would not need to fly as high to be able to cover the same distances.

The concept was known as boost-glide since the first and second stage boosters would carry the payload to its desired altitude, then the payload would glide toward its target.

It had been called the skip-bomber by German rocket scientists during World War II, although the Germans could never thoroughly test the theory. Alpha Draco, on the other hand, successfully tested the technique, which had been studied and refined carefully by the National Advisory Committee for Aeronautics (NACA) well into the 1950's.

In a typical flight profile, the Alpha Draco was launched on a nearly horizontal angle of about 100 degrees. The first stage booster shut down and was jettisoned at an altitude of about 42,000 feet, then the unpowered second stage and payload continued a ballistic trajectory. The second stage fired at an altitude of about 65,000 feet.

The second stage burned out at an altitude of about 92,000 feet about 40 miles downrange of the launch site. The aeroballistic payload, which remained attached to the second stage, then achieved a nearly level glide path, gradually decreasing its altitude until being programmed to begin a terminal dive and impact the ocean about 240 miles downrange of the launch site.

In addition to validating the boost-glide concept, Alpha Draco yielded important data on the aerodynamics of hypersonic flight as well as materials that can withstand high temperatures. The payload employed a pioneering slow roll as it glided to help distribute heat evenly throughout the structure. Although short-lived, the program was valuable in U.S. missile technology evolution.

ATLAS D

Classification: Inter-Continental Ballistic Missile

Length: 82 feet, 6 inches

Diameter: 10 feet

Range: 10,360 miles

Date of First Cape Canaveral Launch: April 14, 1959

Date of Final Cape Canaveral Launch: January 23, 1961

Number of Cape Canaveral Launches: 33

The Atlas D was initially a prototype of the operational Atlas ICBM. Designed for testing of all Atlas operating systems, the Atlas D was eventually placed on active service as the first U.S. ICBM. In point of fact, the U.S. Air Force had begun construction of operational Atlas launch sites before Atlas D test flights were even underway. This was primarily due to a perception among U.S. military leaders that a serious "missile gap" existed between the U.S. and the Soviet Union.

Much stock, so to speak, was placed in the Atlas program from its acceptance. Out of necessity, a decision had been made to prepare for activation of the Atlas ICBM fleet even before the missile had proven itself in flight tests. Construction of launch facilities was underway at the same time flight tests were being conducted to hasten the speed at which the ICBM could be deployed in an operational mode.

The Atlas D was nearly identical to the Atlas C, although the two booster engines were uprated to provide a combined thrust of 367,000 pounds at liftoff, compared to 330,000 pounds for the Atlas C. The thrust of the sustainer engine and vernier engines remained the same. Test-flight profiles for the Atlas D were designed specifically to simulate operational conditions of a deployed and activated ICBM.

The first Atlas D was launched from Cape Canaveral on April 14, 1959. This was followed by Atlas D launches on May 18, 1959 and June 6, 1959. All three of these missiles exploded less than three minutes into their flights. The fourth Atlas D launched from the Cape completed a successful test flight on July 28, 1959. The Atlas D was declared operational on September 9, 1959. Initial deployment of the Atlas ICBM fleet occurred at Vandenberg Air Force Base, California, Offutt Air Force Base, Nebraska and Warren Air Force Base, Wyoming.

The first operational Atlas D missiles were intended to be launched from a vertical storage position on surface-level gantry-serviced launch pads. But to increase safety and security, facilities were modified to allow the Atlas D to be stored horizontally in a concrete surface bunker. The missile could be raised then fueled for a quick launch, which could typically be accomplished in as little as 15 minutes.

Proving itself to be a reliable and versatile launch vehicle, the Atlas D missile became the core booster for Atlas space launch vehicles which would follow. In general terms, Atlas D-based space launch vehicles were classified as Space Launch Vehicle-3 (SLV-3). However, they have historically been better known by the Atlas name in combination with the name of associated upper stages or mission assignments. These variants include the Atlas-Able, Atlas-Agena A, Atlas-Centaur A, Atlas-Centaur B, Atlas-Centaur C and Mercury-Atlas.

HOUND DOG

Classification: Air-to-Surface Cruise Missile

Length: 42 feet, 6 inches

Diameter: 2 feet, 4 inches

Wingspan: 12 feet

Range: 710 miles

Date of First Cape Canaveral Launch: April 23, 1959

Date of Final Cape Canaveral Launch: August 30, 1965

Number of Cape Canaveral Launches: 77

The Hound Dog missile was developed by North American Aviation, later Rockwell International, beginning in 1957.

A bomber-launched air-to-surface winged cruise missile, the Hound Dog was designed to help U.S. manned bombers penetrate enemy airspace. The vehicle also served to fill a cruise missile gap which existed following the cancellation of the Navaho program.

Indeed, the Hound Dog's configuration was adapted directly from the Navaho X-10 test vehicle, which was also built by North American Aviation.

Initially designated AGM-77, the Hound Dog featured small canard foreplanes, rear delta wings with ailerons, plus a small fin and rudder.

The vehicle was powered by a Pratt and Whitney turbojet which could produce a thrust of 7,500 pounds. The engine was located in an underslung rear pod. It featured variable inlet and nozzle systems which could adjust the speed and altitude of the missile.

This allowed the Hound Dog to cruise at altitudes which ranged from tree-top level to 55,000 feet.

Guided by a North American Autonetics Division inertial guidance system which was eventually upgraded to incorporate a Kollsman Star Tracker, the Hound Dog could carry a one-megaton nuclear payload.

The Hound Dog was declared operational at Eglin Air Force Base, Florida in early 1961 for use on the B-52G bomber. When Hound Dog production ceased in 1963, the U.S. Air Force had 593 of the missiles in their inventory.

The deployed Hound Dog missiles were designated AGM-28A, with a slightly improved version designated AGM-28B.

For a time, all U.S. Air Force B-52G and B-52H bombers were equipped with one Hound Dog pylon under each wing. The Hound Dog actually transformed these bombers from eight-engine to ten-engine aircraft at takeoff.

One Hound Dog missile located under each wing was actually ignited at takeoff, providing extra thrust for the bomber itself. The Hound Dog engines were then shut down, and the missiles were re-fueled directly from the B-52's own tanks during flight.

Once re-fueled, the missiles were ready to be fired again and sent on their way, after the proper guidance and target information could be entered and verified.

Filling a vital role in providing a diverse pattern of offensive capabilities for the U.S. Air Force, the Hound Dog was not completely removed from active service until 1976.

BOMARC B

Classification: Surface-to-Air Cruise Missile

Length: 43 feet, 9 inches

Diameter: 2 feet, 11 inches

Wingspan: 18 feet, 2 inches

Range: 440 miles

Date of First Cape Canaveral Launch: May 27, 1959

Date of Final Cape Canaveral Launch: April 15, 1960

Number of Cape Canaveral Launches: 7

Essentially an improved and streamlined Bomarc A, the Bomarc B, designated IM-99B, was ready for flight testing in 1959.

The Bomarc B added a Thiokol solid rocket booster housed under the missile's body. Capable of producing a thrust of 50,000 pounds, the booster fired for 30 seconds before it was jettisoned.

Extra tankage was fashioned within the body of the Bomarc B to house additional JP-4 fuel for two improved Marquardt ramjet engines, each of which had a thrust of 14,000 pounds.

This upgraded propulsion system nearly doubled the range of the Bomarc weapons system. The missile also incorporated a more advanced Westinghouse radar system.

Boeing delivered a total of 349 Bomarc B missiles to the U.S. Air Force between 1961 and 1965. These either replaced aging Bomarc A missiles at existing bases or facilitated Bomarc B deployment at new sites.

New Bomarc B deployments occurred at Kinchloe Air Force Base, Michigan, Duluth Municipal Airport, Minnesota and Niagara Falls Municipal Airport, New York.

In addition, the Royal Canadian Air Force accepted Bomarc B missiles for deployment at bases in North Bay, Ontario and LaMacaza, Quebec.

The last of the Bomarc squadrons was deactivated in 1972.

THOR-ABLE III

Classification: Space Launch Vehicle

Length: 90 feet

Diameter: 8 feet

Date of First Cape Canaveral Launch: August 7, 1959

Date of Final Cape Canaveral Launch: August 7, 1959

Number of Cape Canaveral Launches: 1

Thor-Able III was the NASA designation for a Thor-Able variant configured to support the launch of the Explorer-VI satellite on August 7, 1959. The 143-pound satellite was the first spacecraft to transmit pictures of Earth from space. Thor-Able III employed a Thor missile as first stage, an Aerojet liquid-fueled second stage, an Able solid-fueled third stage and an Atlantic solid-fueled fourth stage.

MACE

Classification: Surface-to-Surface Cruise Missile

Length: 44 feet

Diameter: 4 feet, 6 inches

Wingspan: 22 feet, 11 inches

Mace A Range: 650 miles

Mace B Range: 1,250 miles

Date of First Cape Canaveral Launch: October 29, 1959

Date of Final Cape Canaveral Launch: July 17, 1963

Number of Cape Canaveral Launches: 44

The Mace was a streamlined, more advanced version of the Matador winged cruise missile. Originally designated TM-76, the Mace was designed and built by the Martin Company (later Martin Marietta). Development of the missile began in 1954.

The missile was powered by a turbojet engine which could produce 5,500 pounds of thrust. At launch, boost was provided by a solid-fueled motor attached under the vehicle's tail. The solid rocket booster could produce a thrust of 100,000 pounds.

Mace improvements over the Matador included a lengthened fuselage which doubled the vehicle's fuel capacity. This resulted in increased range and warhead capability.

Mace production began in 1958, and there were ultimately two versions of the missile.

The Mace A, designated TM-76A, carried a Goodyear ATRAN terrain comparison guidance system. Designed to be carried aboard cross-country mobile trailer-launchers, Mace A missiles were deployed in West Germany beginning in June, 1959.

The Mace B, designated TM-76B, carried an AC Sparkplug A-Chiever inertial guidance system. Launched from hardened shelters, Mace B missiles were deployed in Okinawa beginning in 1961. Mace A and Mace B missiles were withdrawn from service by 1966.

ATLAS-ABLE

Classification: Space Launch Vehicle

Length: 97 feet, 9 inches

Diameter: 10 feet

Date of First Cape Canaveral Launch: November 26, 1959

Date of Final Cape Canaveral Launch: December 15, 1960

Number of Cape Canaveral Launches: 3

The Atlas-Able was a four-stage rocket employing the Atlas D missile as its first stage. The vehicle used Able upper stages which were adapted from the Vanguard rocket program.

The second stage was an Aerojet engine with a 7,500-pound thrust. The third stage was an Altair engine with a thrust of 3,000 pounds. A fourth stage injection motor was attached to the payload, and provided a thrust of about 450 pounds.

The Atlas-Able was designed to carry a 1,500-pound payload to low-Earth orbit, a 500-pound payload to lunar impact or a 300-pound payload to Earth-escape trajectory.

The short-lived Atlas-Able was retired in 1960 after it was used in three unsuccessful attempts to send Pioneer spacecraft to the Moon.

PERSHING I

Classification: Medium-Range Ballistic Missile

Length: 34 feet, 10 inches

Diameter: 3 feet, 4 inches

Finspan: 5 feet, 9 inches

Range: 460 miles

Date of First Cape Canaveral Launch: February 25, 1960

Date of Final Cape Canaveral Launch: April 24, 1963

Number of Cape Canaveral Launches: 56

The Pershing program was born in the wake of the "Wilson Memorandum". In 1956, Secretary of Defense Charles E. Wilson stripped the U.S. Army of all missiles with a range of 200 miles or greater.

This policy was rescinded in 1958, which allowed the Army Ballistic Missile Agency (ABMA) to proceed with the development of a solid-fueled missile with a desired range of up to 800 miles.

Named after General "Black Jack" Pershing, a contract for the development of the Pershing missile was granted to the Martin Company (later Martin Marietta) Orlando Division.

This was the first time that the development of a U.S. Army missile was handed over to an industrial contractor. Previously, the ABMA did not grant a production contract until a missile had been fabricated and tested in-house.

Beginning with the Pershing, the U.S. Army followed an established U.S. Air Force pattern of assigning missile development activities directly to military contractors from the time of conception.

Designed as a mobile missile, the first-generation Pershing, called Pershing I, required four vehicles for field deployment. The first vehicle carried the missile itself and an erector launcher.

The second housed a programming test and power station. A third vehicle served as a radio communications terminal center, while the fourth contained the missile's nuclear warhead and azimuth laying equipment.

Prior to launch, the Pershing I was raised vertically, the erector arm was lowered and the missile was fired by remote control.

The Pershing I employed two solid-fueled stages. A Thiokol first stage engine produced 26,290 pounds of thrust and burned for about 39 seconds.

A Thiokol second stage engine produced a 19,220-pound thrust and also burned for about 39 seconds.

An Eclipse Pioneer inertial guidance system directed the Pershing I to its target. The first stage employed three triangular fins, while the second stage employed three rectangular wedge fins to control trajectory during flight.

The inertial guidance system controlled the movement of the fins, which acted as exhaust deflectors to steer the missile. A re-entry vehicle, shaped like a sharply tipped cone, employed ablative technology to deliver the Pershing I weapons payload.

The re-entry vehicle could carry a 400 kiloton nuclear warhead, effectively delivering the equivalent of 400,000 pounds of TNT.

Although this was considered by critics to be an unusually large payload for an MRBM, the capability was established to assure that as much damage as possible would be inflicted should the missile fall short of its intended target.

The first Pershing I test launch occurred on February 24, 1960 from Cape Canaveral. By 1961, all Pershing I test flights were supported by the actual four-vehicle mobile launch system which would be used during field operations.

Declared operational in July, 1962 and designated MGM-31A, Pershing I missiles were deployed in West Germany. A similar version of the Pershing I used strictly for troop training was designated MGM-31B.

ATLAS-AGENA A

Classification: Space Launch Vehicle

Length: 99 feet

Diameter: 10 feet

Date of First Cape Canaveral Launch: February 26, 1960

Date of Final Cape Canaveral Launch: May 24, 1960

Number of Cape Canaveral Launches: 2

The Atlas-Agena A was a two-stage rocket using the Atlas D missile as a first stage and the Lockheed Agena A as a second stage.

The Agena family of second stages originated in the Atlas-Hustler concept proposed by the U.S. Air Force. Since the Agena A was designed to be tailor manufactured for each flight, it proved impractical and was never used by NASA.

The Agena A was 19 feet, 4 inches long and 4 feet, 11 inches wide. It employed a single-start Bell engine producing 15,200 pounds of thrust.

The Bell engine was manufactured in two models for the Agena A. The Model 8001 version burned JP-4 jet fuel while the Model 8048 version burned IRFNA/UDMH liquid fuel.

The total vehicle was capable of carrying a 5,000-pound payload to low-Earth orbit.

THOR-ABLE IV

Classification: Space Launch Vehicle

Length: 90 feet

Diameter: 8 feet

Date of First Cape Canaveral Launch: March 11, 1960

Date of Final Cape Canaveral Launch: March 11, 1960

Number of Cape Canaveral Launches: 1

Thor-Able IV was the NASA designation for a Thor-Able variant configured to support the launch of the Pioneer-V spacecraft on March 11, 1960. The 95-pound spacecraft was successfully sent past the planet Venus and was the world's first spacecraft to send radio signals to Earth from interplanetary distance. The Thor-Able IV employed a Thor missile as first stage, an Aerojet liquid-fueled second stage and an Able solid-fueled third stage.

THOR-ABLE STAR

Classification: Space Launch Vehicle

Length: 79 feet, 4 inches

Diameter: 8 feet

Date of First Cape Canaveral Launch: April 13, 1960

Date of Final Cape Canaveral Launch: October 31, 1962

Number of Cape Canaveral Launches: 11

Introduced in 1960, Thor-Able Star was a two-stage vehicle designed to carry military payloads into orbit.

Employing improved Thor-Able first and second stages and eliminating the weight of additional upper stages, Thor-Able Star was able to carry a maximum 1,000-pound payload into low-Earth orbit.

A Rocketdyne first stage engine burned liquid oxygen/RP-1 (kerosene) liquid fuel and could produce 172,000 pounds of thrust at launch.

An Aerojet second stage engine burned IRFNA/UDMH solid fuel and could produce a 7,730-pound thrust. This upgraded engine could be re-started to augment and adjust the orbit of the payload.

Thor-Able Star was the last version of the Thor-based rockets to be launched from Cape Canaveral carrying the "Thor" name.

In 1960, an improved Thor-based rocket called the Thor-Delta was introduced. The name of this vehicle was officially shortened to Delta in order to distinguish it from military relatives which continued to carry the Thor name.

From this point on, all Thor-based rockets launched from the Cape carried the Delta name only. However, military vehicles carrying the Thor name continued to be launched from Vandenberg Air Force Base, California.

Rockets launched from Vandenberg Air Force Base, California, but never launched from Cape Canaveral, include the Thor-Agena A, Thor-Agena B, Thor-Agena D, Thor-Altair, Thor-Burner II and Thor-Burner IIA.

Indeed, military variants of the Thor-based rockets continued to evolve following the elimination of the Thor name from Cape Canaveral launches. This evolution affected the Delta fleet as well.

The Thrust Augmented Thor (TAT) Agena D was introduced in 1963 by adding three Castor solid rocket boosters to augment the first stage of the Thor-Agena D. This method of thrust augmentation was incorporated into the Delta program beginning with the introduction of the Delta D launch vehicle in 1964.

The TAT-Agena D was later improved by lengthening the first stage fuel tanks. The resulting rocket was called Long Tank Thrust Augmented Thor (LTTAT) Agena D.

The LTTAT-Agena D was alternately referred to by the shortened names Thorad and Long Tank Thor. The vehicle remained in operation until 1972. From 1972 on, military and civilian satellites were both launched on vehicles bearing the Delta name.

It should be noted that although the Thor designation was officially removed from the Delta fleet in 1972, some sources continued to refer to the "Thor-Delta" in reference to Delta launches taking place well beyond that date.

DELTA

Classification: Space Launch Vehicle

Length: 90 feet

Diameter: 8 feet

Date of First Cape Canaveral Launch: May 13, 1960

Date of Final Cape Canaveral Launch: September 18, 1962

Number of Cape Canaveral Launches: 12

Evolving directly from the U.S. Air Force Thor IRBM, the Delta space launch vehicle was designed for NASA in 1959 to handle a variety of satellite payload applications.

Manufactured by Douglas Aircraft, which became McDonnell Douglas, the Delta family gave NASA a firm, reliable foundation for launching intermediate-weight civilian payloads.

Although originally considered a temporary, interim vehicle to meet NASA requirements of that era, the Delta launch vehicle continued to evolve to meet the ever-increasing demands of the civilian and commercial satellite industry, and remains in use today.

The non-military nature of the original Delta vehicle is historically significant, since it was the reason the booster family was given the name it still holds.

The military Thor IRBM had already been adapted for satellite launches prior to the introduction of the Delta vehicle.

The first three Thor-based satellite launchers were called Thor-Able, Thor-Able-Star and Thor-Agena A, based on the respective names of the rocket's upper stage configurations.

The intended name Thor-Delta represented the fourth upper stage configuration for the Thor-based space launch vehicle, because Delta is the fourth letter of the Greek alphabet.

Since the vehicle was designed primarily to be a civilian satellite launcher, the name Thor was eliminated so that the rocket could be better distinguished from its military relatives.

The same basic principle was applied in the late 1950's as the short-lived Redstone MRBM-based and Jupiter IRBM-based rockets were renamed Juno I and Juno II, respectively, for civilian satellite launching applications.

But as far as modern missile-descended rocket families are concerned, the Delta is unique in this regard. The Atlas and Titan rocket families never dropped the names of their military ancestors.

While rockets carrying the Thor name continued to launch military satellites from Vandenberg Air Force Base, California well into the 1970's, the Delta family has served with distinction as one of the longest-lived programs on the Cape.

Introduced in 1960, the original Delta was a three-stage launch vehicle made up of a Thor IRBM mated to improved Vanguard rocket upper stages.

The first stage employed a Rocketdyne engine which burned liquid oxygen/RP-1 (kerosene) liquid fuel and produced a thrust of 150,000 pounds.

An Aerojet-General second stage engine burned IRFNA/UDMH liquid fuel and provided 7,800 pounds of thrust.

The solid-fueled Able third stage motor, adapted from the Vanguard rocket, produced a thrust of 2,800 pounds.

Radio guidance equipment was carried aboard the first and second stages. The third stage was spin-stabilized at 140 r.p.m.

The vehicle could carry a 600-pound payload to low-Earth orbit. It was also designed to carry a 100-pound payload to geostationary transfer orbit, although the first version of the Delta was never used for that purpose.

In a typical flight profile, the first stage was fired at liftoff and burned for about two minutes. After first stage separation at an altitude of nearly 41 miles, the second stage was ignited and burned for about three minutes.

While the second stage burned out as the vehicle coasted to an altitude of about 161.5 miles, the third stage began spinning up to the proper number of revolutions.

Following jettison of the second stage, the third stage was fired for nearly one minute to achieve its necessary orbital velocity.

MERCURY ATLAS

Classification: Space Launch Vehicle

Length: 95 feet, 4 inches

Diameter: 10 feet

Date of First Cape Canaveral Launch: July 29, 1960

Date of Final Cape Canaveral Launch: May 15, 1963

Number of Cape Canaveral Launches: 9

The Mercury-Atlas was essentially an Atlas D missile adapted to carry a NASA Mercury capsule.

The engine thrusts were exactly the same as the operational Atlas D ICBM, with only the flight profile modified to carry the Mercury spacecraft into orbit.

Additional safety features were built into certain Atlas D systems to protect the astronauts. Modifications included incorporation of an Abort Sensing and Implementation System (ASIS). ASIS was designed to protect the astronaut in case of an in-flight emergency.

Other features included improvements in the rate gyro package, range safety system, autopilot, guidance antenna, propellant fill and drain valves, combustion sensors, liquid oxygen turbopump, missile skin width, guidance and engine alignment.

On February 20, 1962 it was a Mercury-Atlas rocket that successfully boosted the MA-6 Friendship 7 capsule with John Glenn aboard. Glenn became the first U.S. astronaut to orbit Earth.

BLUE SCOUT JUNIOR

Classification: Research Rocket

Length: 40 feet, 5 inches

Diameter: 2 feet, 7 inches

Date of First Cape Canaveral Launch: September 21, 1960

Date of Final Cape Canaveral Launch: June 9, 1965

Number of Cape Canaveral Launches: 10

The Scout rocket was conceived in 1958 by NACA, which was exploring the development of a small, lightweight vehicle to launch satellites or perform high-altitude research relatively inexpensively.

The Scout program was assumed by the NASA Langley Research Center upon the creation of the space agency in October, 1958. In less than one year, the Scout design emerged as a four-stage vehicle capable of being used as a sounding rocket or lightweight satellite launcher.

NASA decided that all four stages would be solid-fueled, citing the relative simplicity and reliability of previously demonstrated solid-fuel technology.

In April, 1959, a production contract for the Scout rocket was issued to the Astronautics Division of Ling-Temco-Vought, a subsidiary of the Chance Vought Corporation.

The Scout first stage, called Algor, was controlled by the moveable outer tips of four stabilizer fins in conjunction with four exhaust deflector vanes. It burned for 40 seconds and could produce a thrust of 115,000 pounds.

This first stage concept was applied directly from the U.S. Navy Polaris missile program. The Scout second stage also had its roots in a military program.

The Scout second stage, called Castor, originated with the U.S. Army Sergeant rocket program. It burned for 39 seconds, was stabilized by hydrogen peroxide jets and could produce a thrust of 50,000 pounds.

The Scout third stage, called Antares, was applied from the Vanguard rocket program. The Antares third stage was an upgraded version of the Vanguard Altair third stage.

In its modified form as the Scout third stage, the upgraded Vanguard Altair third stage was simply renamed Antares. It burned for 39 seconds, was stabilized by hydrogen peroxide jets and could produce 13,600 pounds of thrust.

An actual Vanguard Altair third stage was incorporated as the fourth stage of the Scout rocket. The Altair fourth stage burned for 38 seconds, was spin-stabilized and could produce a thrust of 3,000 pounds.

Both the third and fourth stages were encased in a glass-fiber shield which included the payload shroud and a device to spin-stabilize the fourth stage.

The Scout was able to carry a 50-pound payload on a ballistic trajectory to an altitude of 8,500 miles or carry a 150-pound payload into low-Earth orbit.

The original NASA Scout was modified for specific U.S. Air Force applications under the designations Blue Scout I, Blue Scout II and Blue Scout Junior.

The Blue Scout Junior, designated XRM-91, represented a major revision of previous Scout rockets. It was introduced to support smaller, more streamlined scientific research activities of the U.S. Air Force.

The Castor second stage and Antares third stage used on Scout, Blue Scout I and Blue Scout II rockets were adapted to become the first and second stages, respectively, of the Blue Scout Junior.

Each of these stages was modified to carry four fixed, triangular fins at their aft ends. These fins provided stabilization during flight.

A new third stage, called Alcor, was introduced. It burned for 30 seconds and could produce 8,000 pounds of thrust. A new fourth stage, called Cetus, could produce a maximum thrust of 900 pounds.

The rocket, which did not carry any guidance equipment, was launched from a beam used previously for U.S. Army Sergeant missiles. The Blue Scout Junior was spin-stabilized from launch.

Spin rockets on the second stage were fired at launch and stabilized the Blue Scout Junior at three revolutions per second. This motion was sufficient to keep the third and fourth stages on course following burnout of the first two stages.

Launches of all classes of Scout rockets from Cape Canaveral ceased in 1966. However, both the U.S. Air Force and NASA continued to refine the vehicle. The U.S. Air Force introduced the XRM-92, called the Air Force Scout, a four-stage rocket similar to the original NASA Scout.

NASA continued to use a modern version of the Scout for launching lightweight scientific payloads, although all of these launches were conducted from Vandenberg Air Force Base, California.

ATLAS E

Classification: Inter-Continental Ballistic Missile

Length: 82 feet, 6 inches

Diameter: 10 feet

Range: 11,500 miles

Date of First Cape Canaveral Launch: October 11, 1960

Date of Final Cape Canaveral Launch: February 25, 1964

Number of Cape Canaveral Launches: 19

Essentially an upgraded and modified Atlas D missile, the Atlas E carried an uprated propulsion system which increased liftoff thrust by about 8% over the Atlas D and resulted in a greater range for the missile. Another important addition to the Atlas E was an all-inertial guidance system which afforded a significant technical advantage to the operational Atlas ICBM fleet, effectively removing pressure from ground stations during flight.

On July 6, 1961 a Cape-launched Atlas E completed a successful test flight of 9,054 miles. This established a distance record for the Atlas ICBM which was never broken. Atlas E was specifically designed to be housed in underground facilities at Fairchild Air Force Base, Washington, Forbes Air Force Base, Kansas and Warren Air Force Base, Wyoming.

Atlas E missiles were stored horizontally in underground hardened shelters and needed to be raised to a vertical position then fueled prior to launch. These shelters were nicknamed "coffins" and the Atlas E was nicknamed "coffin bird" because the missile was often covered with a thin layer of earth while in storage. Covering the Atlas E missile body with earth, much as an actual coffin would be covered with earth during burial, provided about 25 pounds per square-inch of pressure on the missile body, helping to prevent overpressure when the missile was in storage.

POLARIS A2

Classification: Fleet Ballistic Missile

Note: Fleet Ballistic Missiles are also referred to as Submarine-Launched Ballistic Missiles.

Length: 30 feet, 9 inches

Diameter: 4 feet, 6 inches

Range: 1,727 miles

Date of First Cape Canaveral Launch: November 10, 1960

Date of Final Cape Canaveral Launch: September 2, 1971

Number of Cape Canaveral Launches: 222

Designated UGM-27B, the Polaris A2 was under development in 1959 even before the Polaris A1 had been declared operational.

Based on the basic Polaris A1 design, the Polaris A2 introduced a body which was lengthened about three feet to better fill out the tubes from which it would be launched.

It also carried a new Hercules second stage engine with a glass filament-wound casing, as opposed to steel. This engine employed a rotary nozzle for thrust vector control, as did the Polaris A1 second stage engine.

The Polaris A2 was initially carried aboard all five Ethan Allen Class submarines, which were the first of the Fleet Ballistic Missile (FBM) submarines to be built from scratch.

The next generation of FBM submarines, beginning with SSBN 616 Lafayette, was called the Lafayette Class. The Lafayette Class filled out the initial U.S. Navy FBM fleet of 41 submarines.

Although 31 Lafayette Class submarines were built, only the first eight were outfitted with Polaris A2 missiles. The remainder of the Lafayette Class submarines would eventually be outfitted with improved Polaris A3 and Poseidon missiles.

Polaris A2 missiles remained in service until September, 1974, when the Ethan Allen Class submarine SSBN 611 John Marshall returned to port. Some remaining Polaris A2 missiles were later fired as targets during anti-missile tests.

A Polaris A2 missile held the distinction of being the only FBM ever to carry a live nuclear warhead to its target. In the only FBM test of its kind, a Polaris A2 launched from SSBN 608 Ethan Allen fired a live nuclear warhead toward Christmas Island on May 6, 1962.

MERCURY REDSTONE

Classification: Suborbital Space Launch Vehicle

Length: 83 feet

Diameter: 5 feet, 10 inches

Finspan: 13 feet

Date of First Cape Canaveral Launch: November 21, 1960

Date of Final Cape Canaveral Launch: July 21, 1961

Number of Cape Canaveral Launches: 6

A modified version of the Redstone missile, the Mercury-Redstone was a one-stage rocket used in the initial NASA effort to launch astronauts into space.

In most respects, the Mercury-Redstone was quite similar to its missile relative. The vehicle was, in fact, selected by NASA for the Mercury program because of its proven track record of safety and reliability.

The Mercury-Redstone did incorporate added safety features, as well as an upgraded Rocketdyne A-7 engine. The liquid oxygen/ethyl alcohol liquid-fueled engine was capable of producing 78,000 pounds of thrust at launch.

About 800 engineering changes were made to the production version of the Redstone missile to qualify it as a manned space launch vehicle. These included extending the fuel tank six feet to increase the burn time, thus achieving increased speed and altitude. Other modifications included the addition of an in-flight abort sensing system which would protect the astronaut during an emergency.

Alan Shepard, the first U.S. astronaut, was launched aboard a Mercury-Redstone from Cape Canaveral Launch Pad 5 on May 5, 1961 on mission MR-3. A nearly identical flight designated MR-4 featuring astronaut Virgil "Gus" Grissom was conducted on July 21, 1961.

Mercury-Redstone mission performance in support of suborbital manned flights MR-3 and MR-4 was so successful that two similar flights which would have been designated MR-5 and MR-6 were cancelled.

BLUE SCOUT I

Classification: Space Launch Vehicle

Length: 71 feet, 11 inches

Diameter: 3 feet, 4 inches

Date of First Cape Canaveral Launch: January 7, 1961

Date of Final Cape Canaveral Launch: April 12, 1962

Number of Cape Canaveral Launches: 3

In 1960, the NASA Scout was modified in support of U.S. Air Force activities. The Blue Scout I, carrying a numerical designation of XRM-89, was the first military version of the Scout rocket.

In all other respects identical to the NASA Scout, the Blue Scout I eliminated the Altair fourth stage. Removal of the fourth stage left room to accommodate a larger and heavier payload than could have been carried otherwise.

As a three-stage launcher, the Blue Scout I was able to carry a 400-pound payload into low-Earth orbit.

MINUTEMAN I

Classification: Inter-Continental Ballistic Missile

LGM-30A Minuteman I Length: 54 feet

LGM-30B Minuteman I Length: 55 feet, 9 inches

Diameter of Both: 6 feet, 4 inches

Range of Both: 6,214 miles

Date of First Cape Canaveral Launch: February 1, 1961

Date of Final Cape Canaveral Launch: September 29, 1964

Number of Cape Canaveral Launches: 54

The Minuteman ICBM resulted from studies which began in 1956. At the time, the U.S. Air Force sought to determine the feasibility of deploying a land-based, solid-fueled IRBM.

While development work on the U.S. Air Force Thor IRBM and U.S. Army Jupiter IRBM was already well underway, these were both liquid-fueled missiles which were considered to require high-maintenance.

A solid-fueled missile could remain stored for long periods of time, requiring little maintenance and no fueling prior to launch. It could also be safely housed in underground silos, providing a dramatic tactical advantage over the surface-based Thor and Jupiter.

The solid-fueled IRBM originated as Project Q, then Weapons System 133 (WS-133) and finally SM-80, dubbed Minuteman after the Revolutionary War soldier who could be ready to fire a shot in less than a minute.

A proposal for the Minuteman missile was accepted by the U.S. Air Force from Boeing in 1958. Since a three-stage version of this missile could achieve a range in excess of 6,000 miles, the Minuteman was subsequently reclassified as an ICBM.

While proposals existed for creating MRBM and IRBM versions of the Minuteman by mixing and matching the first, second and third stages, these were never actually produced.

The Minuteman provided the U.S. Air Force with a smaller, less expensive ICBM which was much less labor-intensive than its liquid-fueled counterparts and could be launched quickly at the push of a button.

The first generation of the Minuteman was deployed under the LGM-30A designation, with an improved version designated LGM-30B. These missiles are more commonly referred to as the Minuteman I.

The Minuteman I first stage employed a Thiokol engine which burned PBAA polymer binder, AP oxidant and aluminum powder. The first stage engine could produce a thrust of 200,000 pounds at liftoff.

An Aerojet-General second stage engine burned PU/AP fuel and provided a 60,000-pound thrust.

A Hercules third stage engine burned Nc/Ng/AP fuel and produced a thrust of 35,000 pounds.

All three stages were housed within a steel frame, although certain frame sections were later replaced with titanium.

Each stage employed gimbaled exhaust nozzles. This marked the first time gimbaled exhaust nozzles were used on solid-fueled engines.

The Minuteman I was controlled by an Autonetics inertial guidance system. An advanced design in its day, the Autonetics system was the first to employ solid state technology, sub-miniature digital computer hardware and integrated circuit microelectronics.

An Avco re-entry nosecone could carry a 1.3 megaton warhead. The Minuteman I was initially designed to be launched from a mobile railway system as well as underground silos. The railway option was abandoned prior to actual Minuteman I testing and deployment.

Before the two Minuteman test silos were completed at Cape Canaveral, the missiles were launched from simplified facilities that could best be described as a "hole in the ground".

While not yet considered full silo-based launches, Minuteman I missiles launched under these early underground conditions did produce the characteristic "smoke ring" that became a Minuteman trademark during launches from silos.

The first full-silo Minuteman I launch from Cape Canaveral occurred in 1961. The missile blew up in the silo, creating one of the most memorable and spectacular failures in the history of the Cape.

Minuteman I missiles were deployed in operational wings which occupied large expanses of land. Tactical rules dictated that launch control facilities be separated by at least 11 miles, with each silo separated by at least 4 miles.

Each silo was 80 feet deep and 12 feet wide. The silos were lined with steel and accessible from two adjacent equipment rooms located 28 feet underground.

Remarkably, the Minuteman I wings could remain largely unmanned. Just two officers located in distant firing rooms were responsible for each grouping of ten missile silos.

The Minuteman I became operational in December, 1962 with a partial deployment of LGM-30A missiles at Malstrom Air Force Base, Montana. This was designated Wing I, with deployment of 150 missiles supporting three squadrons of five ten-missile groups completed in July, 1963.

Identical deployment of 150 LGM-30A missiles each was subsequently completed at Ellsworth Air Force Base, South Dakota (Wing II), Minot Air Force Base, North Dakota (Wing III) and Whiteman Air Force Base, Missouri (Wing IV).

Minuteman I production was switched to the LGM-30B for deployment at Warren Air Force Base, Wyoming (Wing V). The LGM-30B was slightly longer than the LGM-30A, featured a titanium second stage frame and employed an improved Avco re-entry vehicle.

Wing V supported one additional Minuteman I squadron, for a total of four. As a result, 200 missiles were deployed at Warren Air Force Base. With 600 missiles already located at Wings I through IV, Minuteman I deployment reached a total of 800 by June, 1965.

BLUE SCOUT II

Classification: Research Rocket

Length: 71 feet, 11 inches

Diameter: 3 feet, 4 inches

Date of First Cape Canaveral Launch: March 3, 1961

Date of Final Cape Canaveral Launch: April 12, 1961

Number of Cape Canaveral Launches: 2

Representing the second U.S. Air Force variant of the NASA Scout, the Blue Scout II carried a numerical designation of XRM-90.

The Blue Scout II carried the same four-stage array as the original NASA Scout. However, the stages were improved so that the Blue Scout II could carry a 365-pound payload on a ballistic trajectory to an altitude of 8,500 miles.

ATLAS F

Classification: Inter-Continental Ballistic Missile

Length: 82 feet, 6 inches

Diameter: 10 feet

Range: 11,500 miles

Date of First Cape Canaveral Launch: August 8, 1961

Date of Final Cape Canaveral Launch: April 1, 1964

Number of Cape Canaveral Launches: 14

The Atlas F was the final and most advanced version of the Atlas ICBM and was essentially a quick-firing version of the Atlas E, modified to be stored in a vertical position inside underground concrete and steel silos. When stored, the Atlas F sat atop an elevator. If a missile was placed on alert, it was fueled with RP-1 (kerosene) liquid fuel, which could be stored inside the missile for extended periods. If a decision was made to launch the missile, it was fueled with liquid oxygen. Once the liquid oxygen fueling was complete, the elevator raised the missile to the surface for launching.

This method of storage allowed the Atlas F to be launched in about ten minutes, a saving of about five minutes over the Atlas D and Atlas E, both of which were stored horizontally and had to be raised to a vertical position before being fueled with either RP-1 (kerosene) liquid fuel or liquid oxygen. Atlas F missiles were deployed at Schilling Air Force Base, Kansas, Plattsburg Air Force Base, New York, Lincoln Air Force Base, Nebraska, Altus Air Force Base, Oklahoma, Dyess Air Force Base, Texas and Walker Air Force Base, New Mexico.

ATLAS-AGENA B

Classification: Space Launch Vehicle

Length: 98 feet

Diameter: 10 feet

Date of First Cape Canaveral Launch: August 23, 1961

Date of Final Cape Canaveral Launch: June 6, 1966

Number of Cape Canaveral Launches: 12

Using the Atlas E or Atlas F missile as a first stage, the Atlas-Agena B featured an improved version of the Agena A as second stage.

The Agena B was 23 feet, 7 inches long and 4 feet, 11 inches wide. It employed one Bell engine capable of producing a thrust of 16,000 pounds.

Both the Model 8081 and Model 8096 versions of the Agena B engine burned IRFNA/UDMH liquid fuel. The Agena B was the first Agena to have multiple re-start capability, which added great versatility to its satellite applications.

The entire vehicle was designed to carry a 5,780-pound payload to low-Earth orbit, a 750-pound payload to Earth-escape trajectory or a 450-pound payload to a Mars or Venus trajectory.

SATURN I BLOCK I

Classification: Space Launch Vehicle

Length: 164 feet

Diameter: 21 feet, 6 inches

Date of First Cape Canaveral Launch: October 27, 1961

Date of Final Cape Canaveral Launch: March 28, 1963

Number of Cape Canaveral Launches: 4

Conceived as an element of the short-lived Juno class of space launch vehicles, the rocket which would become the Saturn I was born on the drawing boards of the Army Ballistic Missile Agency (ABMA) in 1957.

At the time, an ABMA design team led by Wernher von Braun envisioned a heavy lift rocket with a powerful first stage made up of a cluster of eight Redstone missile stages surrounding one Jupiter missile stage. The pioneering clustered engine concept was referred to by critics as "cluster's last stand" because some believed the resulting rocket would not be able to get off the ground.

Each of these clustered stages was to be fitted with a Rocketdyne engine adapted from the U.S. Air Force Thor missile program. The nine-engine first stage array would be capable of producing about 1.5 million pounds of thrust at liftoff.

This design represented the first attempt to increase a rocket's payload capacity by clustering existing missile stages. The ABMA had indeed presented an extremely challenging and advanced rocket concept with far-reaching implications for the future of space flight.

In August, 1958, the Advanced Research Projects Agency (ARPA) issued an official authorization for the ABMA to develop a rocket with a clustered first stage under the designation Juno V.

Redstone-based Juno I and Jupiter-based Juno II rockets had already been successfully developed. Although concept vehicles known as Juno III and Juno IV were also under active review at the time, development of these rockets never occurred.

There was a possibility that the eight Redstone stages and one Jupiter stage which made up the Juno V first stage array could have been used simply as fuel tanks to feed four upgraded Rocketdyne engines, each of which could produce 330,000 pounds of thrust at launch.

However, a decision was made to continue Juno V development using Rocketdyne Thor engines as originally conceived. Rocketdyne later introduced a more simplified and compact new engine called the H-1 which was actually employed in operational vehicles.

The large size of the rocket became an engineering challenge at the outset. It was originally proposed that the clustered first stage tanks be manufactured separately from the main body of the vehicle, then attached to the main body at the launch site.

This design was considered due to the limitations of transport aircraft at the time, which could not accommodate a payload more than ten feet in diameter. Further review indicated it would take as many as 11 C-124 aircraft flights to transport the rocket components from Huntsville, Alabama to Cape Canaveral for each vehicle, which was deemed inefficient and overly expensive.

Attaching the individual clusters at the launch site was also considered to be too time consuming and risky. In the end, the rocket was manufactured with all of its component clusters affixed to the main vehicle body, with the entire first stage transported from Huntsville to Cape Canaveral by barge. These were the first rocket components to be transported to Cape Canaveral in this manner.

In October, 1958, Wernher von Braun suggested that the Juno V be renamed Saturn. Since the rocket was dramatically different from the Jupiter-based Juno II, he felt the name was appropriate since the planet Saturn is the next "step" away from the planet Jupiter.

The ARPA approved the name change on February 3, 1959. Later that year, another significant change was in store. On October 21, 1959 the ABMA Development Operations Division, including the Saturn rocket program and Wernher von Braun, was transferred to NASA.

This was the logical direction for the Saturn program to take. Although the Army had conceived and designed the vehicle, they had no application in which to use it. Although the Army had proposed several of its own rather fanciful manned space flight programs which could employ the Saturn rocket, these programs never materialized after a civilian space program emerged.

NASA, on the other hand, had already embarked on an ambitious manned space flight program, which was intended to send men to the Moon and back at some point in the near future. Since the Army had a rocket with no program and NASA had a program with no rocket, NASA inherited the Saturn program intact.

With the ultimate configuration of Saturn rockets still in the design stage, a government Saturn Vehicle Evaluation Committee, known as the Silverstein Committee, recommended that NASA consider three options for the vehicle.

These options were called Saturn A, Saturn B and Saturn C. These represented a hodgepodge of heavy lift vehicle options using a wide array of upper stage configurations based on existing technology, built around the Army clustered first stage concept.

Of these, the Saturn C option was selected. Five versions of the Saturn C, numbered Saturn C-1 through Saturn C-5, ranging from the least powerful to the most powerful, were proposed.

It should be noted that sources differ on the specific meaning of the "C" designation. Some sources refer to the "C" as standing for "configuration" or "concept" but the best information suggests that "C" was simply the third Saturn design option considered by the Silverstein Committee. Hence, the third design option was simply represented by the third letter of the alphabet.

As proposed, the Saturn C-1, already well under development, would be a two-stage vehicle which closely followed original plans for the Juno V. The Saturn C-2 would employ the Saturn C-1 first stage, plus an improved second stage and added third stage.

The three-stage Saturn C-3 would employ two powerful new Rocketdyne F-1 engines in its first stage. The three-stage Saturn C-4 would employ four F-1 engines in its first stage, and the three-stage Saturn C-5 would employ an array of five F-1 engines in its first stage.

However, not all of these vehicles were actually developed. In June, 1961 NASA canceled plans to incorporate an optional third stage on the Saturn C-1. At the same time, a decision was made to use the two-stage Saturn C-1 for Apollo research and development flights.

A proposed uprated version of the Saturn C-1, called the Saturn C-1B, could meet future NASA requirements by employing improved engines. Development of the Saturn C-2, Saturn C-3 and Saturn C-4 vehicles was discontinued. Development of the Saturn C-5 continued.

This more streamlined and cost-effective development plan would be essential if NASA hoped to meet President John F. Kennedy's announced goal of sending men to the Moon and back by the end of the 1960's.

With veteran Redstone and Jupiter producer Chrysler serving as prime contractor, the Saturn C-1 was readied for flight testing by 1961. Flight tests occurred in configurations called Block I and Block II.

In the Block I configuration, a live first stage was flown. A dummy second stage, made up of an inert Jupiter missile shell ballasted with water, was attached atop the first stage to provide aerodynamic stability.

As per Juno V design plans, the Saturn C-1 first stage was made up of eight Redstone stages surrounding one Jupiter stage. But unlike the original plans for the Juno V, these stages acted as fuel tanks only, and did not contain engines at the base of each.

A total of eight Rocketdyne H-1 engines were employed in the first stage, which was called S-1. These were located at the base of the Saturn C-I in two squares of four engines each.

Four of the H-1 engines comprised a tight square at the center of the rocket's base. The remaining four H-1 engines were located on outside "corners" of the base, creating the appearance that one larger square of engines surrounded a smaller square of engines.

Four of the Redstone stages and the Jupiter stage contained liquid oxygen. The remaining four Redstone stages carried RP-1 (kerosene) liquid fuel. A combination of these fuels fed the eight H-1 engines.

The first four Saturn I vehicles were launched in the Block I configuration, employing a first stage capable of producing a thrust of about 1,330,000 pounds at launch. These launches were chiefly intended to test the flight dynamics of the vehicle and the reliability of the first stage clustered configuration.

The Saturn C-1 was renamed Saturn I in February, 1963 prior to the vehicle's fourth test flight. The "C" was also dropped from the other Saturn rockets, which became Saturn IB and Saturn V.

As a result, even Saturn C-1 launches which occurred prior to the name change are now referred to as Saturn I.

MERCURY SCOUT

Classification: Space Launch Vehicle

Length: 71 feet, 11 inches

Diameter: 3 feet, 4 inches

Date of First Cape Canaveral Launch: November 1, 1961

Date of Final Cape Canaveral Launch: November 1, 1961

Number of Cape Canaveral Launches: 1

On May 5, 1961, the same day the first U.S. astronaut was launched, NASA issued a document that proposed the use of Scout rockets to evaluate the Mercury tracking and real-time computer network in preparation for manned orbital missions.

The proposal was approved on May 24, 1961 and on June 13, 1961 the NASA Space Task Group issued detailed technical instrumentation requirements for the modified Scout rocket, which became known as Mercury-Scout.

Each Mercury-Scout rocket would be required to carry a lightweight communications payload into Earth-orbit to allow a simulation of the tracking of an actual orbiting Mercury capsule through the Mercury global network.

A decision was made to modify Blue Scout II number D-8 for the first, and what would be the last, Mercury-Scout mission. The launch would be conducted by the U.S. Air Force, which had already begun launching Blue Scout rockets at Cape Canaveral.

The Mercury-Scout, performing mission MS-1, was launched on November 1, 1961 from Cape Canaveral Launch Pad 18B. The rocket developed erratic flight 28 seconds after being launched, and was destroyed by the Range Safety Officer after 43 seconds of flight.

Mercury program managers subsequently decided that additional missions of Mercury-Scout rockets were not necessary. By the end of 1961, Mercury-Atlas missions MA-4 and MA-5 had already demonstrated that actual orbiting Mercury capsules could be successfully tracked.

TITAN II

Classification: Inter-Continental Ballistic Missile

Length: 102 feet

Diameter: 10 feet

Range: 9,325 miles

Date of First Cape Canaveral Launch: March 16, 1962

Date of Final Cape Canaveral Launch: April 9, 1964

Number of Cape Canaveral Launches: 23

The largest missile ever deployed by the United States, the Titan II also logged distinguished service as the core booster for the NASA Gemini manned space flight program.

Following the Soviet launch of Sputnik I on October 4, 1957, U.S. military officials confirmed that their "cold war" adversary possessed potent ICBM technology. Clearly, the U.S. would need to meet this threat with ICBM technology surpassing that of the Atlas and Titan I.

In 1958, the Martin Company (later Martin Marietta) proposed an improved version of the Titan I which would burn fuels that could remain stored in the missile's fuel tanks for long periods of time. This effectively made the missile ready for near-immediate launches, since the need for pre-launch fueling operations would be eliminated.

The U.S. Air Force granted a development contract to the Martin Company in late 1958. A production contract followed in June, 1960. The resulting ICBM was designated SM-68B and named Titan II. The missile was vastly more advanced than the Titan I.

Aerojet-General first and second stage engines based on those of the Titan I were modified to burn a combination of unsymmetrical dimethyl hydrazine (UDMH) as fuel and nitrogen tetroxide as oxidizer.

These fuels could be stored at room temperature for months with neither evaporation nor corrosion. And, since these fuels were hypergolic, or ignited when they came into contact with each other, the Titan II did not need to employ a complex ignition system.

The Titan II first stage employed an Aerojet-General twin-chambered engine, with each individual chamber capable of producing a 216,000-pound thrust. An Aerojet-General second stage engine could produce a thrust of 100,000 pounds.

Designed to be launched from the bottom of an underground silo, each Titan II could be readied for launch in under 60 seconds.

A pure inertial guidance system from AC Sparkplug and IBM controlled the Titan II in flight. A GE re-entry vehicle could carry an 18 megaton warhead, providing nearly five times the destructive capability of the Titan I.

The first Titan II was launched on March 16, 1962 and the entire missile system met all of its test objectives. The Titan II was declared operational in 1963 under the numerical designation LGM-25C.

A total of 54 Titan II missiles were deployed in six separate squadrons each responsible for nine missiles.

Two squadrons were located at Davis-Monthan Air Force Base, Arizona, two were located at Little Rock Air Force Base, Arkansas while two squadrons were located at McConnell Air Force Base, Kansas.

With a relatively long life as a weapons system, the Titan II fleet was continuously maintained and upgraded through the early 1980's. Deactivation of the Titan II fleet began in 1982, and was completed by 1987.

Remaining Titan II missiles were modified for unmanned space flight as the Titan II-B and Titan II-G. Neither of these were ever launched from Cape Canaveral.

However, early in its career, the Titan II was modified to act as a core booster for the NASA Gemini program.

SKYBOLT

Classification: Air-Launched Ballistic Missile

Length: 38 feet, 3 inches

Diameter: 2 feet, 11 inches

Finspan: 5 feet, 6 inches

Range: 1,150 miles

Date of First Cape Canaveral Launch: April 19, 1962

Date of Final Cape Canaveral Launch: December 22, 1962

Number of Cape Canaveral Launches: 6

Development of the Skybolt Air-Launched Ballistic Missile began in 1958 following feasibility studies to determine whether or not a ballistic-type missile could be successfully deployed from the air.

Since fixed land-based missiles were prone to attack, a ballistic missile which could be dropped from high altitude then guided toward its target proved to be strategically desirable.

Although the Skybolt did have wings, it was originally classified as an Air Launched Ballistic Missile (ALBM), not a cruise missile. It did, however, bear great resemblance to cruise missiles which followed, and has been classified by some as a cruise missile.

The U.S. Air Force requested ALBM design proposals from the aerospace industry in 1959. Douglas Aircraft was selected to begin development studies under the designation Weapons System-138A (WS-138A) Missile GAM-87, called Skybolt.

Guidance for the Skybolt was assigned to Northrup Nortronics, while the propulsion system was assigned to Aerojet-General. An advanced GE re-entry vehicle was selected to carry the Skybolt weapons payload.

A full development contract for the Skybolt was granted to Douglas Aircraft in 1960. The first high-altitude drop testing of inert Skybolt missile bodies began in 1961 over the Gulf of Mexico.

The Skybolt was ultimately intended to be deployed on B-52H aircraft, which were fitted with two twin Skybolt pylons under each inner wing. In this configuration, each aircraft could carry a total of eight missiles.

Following several failures during early flight testing, the Skybolt program was abruptly cancelled on December 19, 1962. Ironically, a Skybolt missile completed a flawless test flight on the same day the program was cancelled.

The Skybolt cancellation was brought about by several prevailing factors. By 1961, the U.S. military was already at a point of deploying several other reliable land, sea and aircraft-based nuclear weapons systems.

In addition, certain engineering elements of the Skybolt were thought to be too complicated to be effectively applied. The early failures added to this concern.

However, the final decision may have been based largely on economics. The British government was faced with a decision of purchasing from the U.S. either air-based Skybolt or sea-based Polaris missiles to augment their national defense arsenal.

The British chose to purchase Polaris missiles, thus eliminating a viable source of funding for the U.S. government to continue refining the Skybolt for eventual deployment.

Test flights of Skybolt missiles for research purposes continued following the official cancellation of the program.

ATLAS-CENTAUR 1962

Classification: Space Launch Vehicle

Length: 105 feet

Diameter: 10 feet

Date of First Cape Canaveral Launch: May 8, 1962

Date of Final Cape Canaveral Launch: August 11, 1965

Number of Cape Canaveral Launches: 6

The name Atlas-Centaur has come to be applied as a generic name for a variety of Atlas-based first and upper stage combinations which evolved from the Atlas D and remained in use for many years.

The first Atlas-Centaur, introduced in 1962, employed the Atlas D missile as first stage and the Convair-developed Centaur as second stage. The Centaur was originally designed to support the launch of the Advent geostationary communications satellite.

The original Centaur, called Centaur A, employed two Pratt and Whitney engines which produced a total thrust of 30,000 pounds. The Centaur engines burned a combination of liquid oxygen and liquid hydrogen.

Improved Centaur second stages designated Centaur B and Centaur C were all initially flown in a similar configuration prior to the debut of an upgraded Atlas-Centaur launch vehicle in 1966.

For this reason, early Atlas-Centaur rockets may more accurately be referred to as Atlas-Centaur A, Atlas-Centaur B or Atlas-Centaur C, depending on the type of Centaur upper stage flown.

POLARIS A3

Classification: Fleet Ballistic Missile

Note: Fleet Ballistic Missiles are also referred to as Submarine-Launched Ballistic Missiles.

Length: 32 feet, 4 inches

Diameter: 4 feet, 6 inches

Range: 2,880 miles

Date of First Cape Canaveral Launch: August 7, 1962

Date of Final Cape Canaveral Launch: February 20, 1979

Number of Cape Canaveral Launches: 194

The third and final generation of the Polaris missile, the Polaris A3, was under development in 1960. Designated UGM-27C, the missile was considerably more advanced and had a much longer life than its two ancestors.

The Polaris A3 featured a full-diameter re-entry vehicle, which gave the missile a more streamlined appearance than the heavily tapered, small-nosed Polaris A1 and Polaris A2.

It also employed a new high-energy Hercules second stage engine which burned Nc/Ng/AP solid propellant and featured a freon fluid injection thrust vector control.

For the first time, both the first and second stage engines were housed in glass filament-wound casings as opposed to steel. Only the Polaris A2 second stage had previously used the glass filament-wound casing.

A GE inertial guidance system coupled with a GE fire control provided an on-board guidance package that was 60 percent lighter than similar hardware used on the Polaris A1 and A2.

In addition to outfitting U.S. Lafayette Class submarines, Polaris A3 missiles were deployed aboard the British submarines HMS Resolution, HMS Renown, HMS Repulse and HMS Revenge by the mid-1970's. The British subsequently renamed their Polaris A3 missiles "Chevaline".

A total of 1,409 Polaris missiles were manufactured, including the Polaris A1, A2 and A3. Although Polaris A3 production ceased in June, 1968 the missile continued to be upgraded as necessary.

As initially deployed, the Polaris A3 carried a Lockheed re-entry vehicle outfitted with a single 500-kiloton nuclear warhead, as in previous Polaris applications.

In the early 1970's, the re-entry vehicle was redesigned to hold three separate, maneuverable 200-kiloton warheads. Although these warheads could not be independently targeted, they were able to impact up to (800 meters) away from each other.

In 1974, the British Polaris A3 (Chevaline) missiles were improved so that each one could carry a total of six independently targeted, maneuverable 40-kiloton warheads. These warheads could impact up to (70 kilometers) away from each other.

The U.S. Navy Polaris A3 missiles were withdrawn from service in February, 1982. The British Polaris A3 (Chevaline) missiles remained in service until the mid-1980's.

DELTA A

Classification: Space Launch Vehicle

Length: 90 feet

Diameter: 8 feet

Date of First Cape Canaveral Launch: October 2, 1962

Date of Final Cape Canaveral Launch: October 27, 1962

Number of Cape Canaveral Launches: 2

Nearly identical to the original Delta, the Delta A carried an upgraded Rocketdyne first stage engine capable of increasing the first stage thrust to 172,500 pounds.

This allowed the Delta A to carry a 700-pound payload to low-Earth orbit. The vehicle was also designed to carry a 150-pound payload to geostationary transfer orbit, although it was never used for that purpose.

DELTA B

Classification: Space Launch Vehicle

Length: 92 feet, 11 inches

Diameter: 8 feet

Date of First Cape Canaveral Launch: December 13, 1962

Date of Final Cape Canaveral Launch: March 19, 1964

Number of Cape Canaveral Launches: 10

In most respects, the Delta B was very similar to the Delta A which preceded it, but featured an improved second stage.

The second stage propellant tanks were lengthened 35.8 inches to increase the amount of fuel they could carry. An upgraded Aerojet-General second stage engine, coupled with this additional fuel capacity, facilitated the launch of heavier payloads.

The Delta B also incorporated an improved guidance and electronics system.

The vehicle was capable of carrying an 825-pound payload to low-Earth orbit, or a 150-pound payload to geostationary transfer orbit.

It was a Delta B rocket that supported the deployment of the world's first geosynchronous satellite.

SYNCOM-1, launched aboard a Delta B on February 14, 1963, achieved a near-synchronous orbit. This was followed by the launch of SYNCOM-2 aboard a Delta B on July 26, 1963. SYNCOM-2 was the first satellite to achieve geosynchronous orbit.

THOR-ASSET

Classification: Research Rocket

Length: 71 feet

Diameter: 8 feet

Date of First Cape Canaveral Launch: September 18, 1963

Date of Final Cape Canaveral Launch: February 23, 1965

Number of Cape Canaveral Launches: 6

Thor Asset was a Thor ballistic missile fitted atop with an ASSET payload. ASSET, or Aerothermodynamic elastic Structural Systems Environmental Tests, was an Air Force program intended to test characteristics of a high-speed re-entry vehicle. The ASSET program investigated the effects of vibration and temperature changes on the shape and materials of experimental hypersonic flight craft which employed a glide concept of re-entry.

Six delta-winged ASSET vehicles were built by the McDonnell Company. Each was 6 feet long with a diameter of 5 feet, 6 inches weighing 1,000 to 1,200 pounds. Each was small enough to be launched atop a Thor missile yet large enough to produce useable aerodynamic data in flight. ASSET vehicles were built in two types: the ASSET ASV, or aerothermodynamic structural vehicles, and the ASSET AEV, or aerothermoelastic vehicles. The ASV investigated temperature and pressure effects, while the AEV investigated responses to forces within the atmosphere.

At the moment of separation from the Thor missile booster, the ASSET vehicles achieved a speed of anywhere from Mach 12 to Mach 19 at altitudes of 200,000 feet. During the glide toward Earth, cold gas reaction systems controlled the path of the vehicles. Data was telemetered to ground stations. The ASSET program yielded valuable hypersonic flight data which was applied to a number of programs intended to validate the precise re-entry and landing of orbiting spaceplanes.

ATLAS-AGENA D

Classification: Space Launch Vehicle

Length: 102 feet

Diameter: 10 feet

Date of First Cape Canaveral Launch: October 16, 1963

Date of Final Cape Canaveral Launch: April 6, 1978

Number of Cape Canaveral Launches: 35

With either an Atlas E or Atlas F missile as a first stage, the Atlas-Agena D featured an improved version of the Agena second stage.

The Agena D was derived directly from the Agena B, with specific modifications made to accommodate a greater variety of payloads. Most notably, the Agena D was used as a target vehicle for manned Gemini rendezvous and docking missions.

The same size as the Agena B, the Agena D was powered by a multiple re-start Bell engine. The engine burned nitrogen tetroxide/UDMH liquid fuel and could produce 16,000 pounds of thrust.

The total vehicle was designed to carry a 5,980-pound payload to low-Earth orbit, an 850-pound payload to Earth-escape trajectory or a 550-pound payload to a Mars or Venus trajectory.

SATURN I BLOCK II

Classification: Space Launch Vehicle

Length: 190 feet, 4 inches

Diameter: 21 feet, 6 inches

Finspan: 18 feet

Date of First Cape Canaveral Launch: January 29, 1964

Date of Final Cape Canaveral Launch: July 30, 1965

Number of Cape Canaveral Launches: 6

The first four Saturn I test launches were in the Block I configuration. The fifth Saturn I test launch onward employed the Block II configuration, which featured an operational first and second stage.

The Saturn I second stage, called S-IV, was powered by a Pratt and Whitney engine which could produce a 90,000-pound thrust. The engine burned liquid oxygen/liquid hydrogen fuel. The S-IV second stage was used to support a variety of Apollo flight test objectives.

In the Block II configuration, the Saturn I employed lengthened fuel tanks and improved H-1 engines. This combination increased the first stage thrust to about 1,520,000 pounds at launch. The Block II configuration also added eight stabilization fins to the base of the first stage, four small stubby fins and four large fins which each extended about 9 feet from the first stage.

An operational Saturn I was capable of carrying a 37,900-pound payload into low-Earth orbit.

Since additional performance improvements were necessary to facilitate NASA objectives for the Apollo program, the Saturn I was eventually replaced by the more powerful Saturn IB.

GEMINI TITAN II

Classification: Space Launch Vehicle

Length: 109 feet

Diameter: 10 feet

Date of First Cape Canaveral Launch: April 8, 1964

Date of Final Cape Canaveral Launch: November 11, 1966

Number of Cape Canaveral Launches: 12

Nearly identical in performance characteristics to the Titan II ICBM, the Gemini-Titan II incorporated a number of safety modifications prior to being used as a core booster for the NASA Gemini manned space flight program.

In the Gemini-Titan II first stage LR87-AJ7 engine burned Aerozine 50/Nitrogen Tetroxide liquid fuel and could produce a liftoff thrust of 430,000 pounds. The LR91-AJ7 second stage engine also burned Aerozine 50/Nitrogen Tetroxide liquid fuel and could produce a thrust of 100,000 pounds.

Safety modifications included the incorporation of a Gemini Malfunction Detection System to inform the crew of the rocket's status and improve response time in an emergency. Redundant systems were built in to reduce the chances of an in-flight malfunction. The inertial guidance system was replaced with a lighter weight radio ground guidance system. The avionics truss in the second stage was slightly modified.

In addition, the second stage propellant tanks were lengthened to provide additional burn time. Unnecessary vernier engines and retro-rockets were removed. The first stage was loaded with 13,000 pounds of fuel more than that of the Titan II ICBM, even though the tank size remained unchanged. Modifications were made to the tracking, electrical and hydraulics systems to improve reliability. The propellants were chilled slightly to improve performance. First stage engine thrust was reduced slightly to cut down on vibration and gravity loads. The first stage was designed to cut off at fuel depletion, as opposed to the Titan II ICBM whose first stage cut off before fuel was depleted.

Overall vehicle performance was sufficient to support the entire Gemini program, although there were a number of problems with the rocket that cropped up and needed to be troubleshooted as the program continued.

ATLAS-ANTARES

Classification: Suborbital Research Rocket

Length: 82 feet, 6 inches

Diameter: 10 feet

Date of First Cape Canaveral Launch: April 14, 1964

Date of Final Cape Canaveral Launch: May 22, 1965

Number of Cape Canaveral Launches: 2

The Atlas Antares rocket consisted of an Atlas D missile as first stage mated to an Antares second stage. The rocket was used in support of the NASA Project FIRE, standing for Flight Investigation of Re-entry. Project FIRE 1 was launched from Cape Canaveral on April 14, 1964, while Project FIRE 2 was launched from the Cape on May 22, 1965.

The Project FIRE payload consisted of an instrumented cone styled as a miniature Project Apollo space capsule, designed to mimic the re-entry characteristics of proposed Apollo re-entry vehicle. Particular attention was paid to the temperature and thermal characteristics of the re-entry vehicle. The two flights were suborbital, with the payload launched into space and then pointed downward for an unpowered re-entry through the atmosphere. Results were important to the upcoming Apollo program.

111

DELTA D

Classification: Space Launch Vehicle

Length: 92 feet, 11 inches

Diameter: 8 feet

Date of First Cape Canaveral Launch: August 19, 1964

Date of Final Cape Canaveral Launch: April 6, 1965

Number of Cape Canaveral Launches: 2

Originally called the Thrust Augmented Delta (TAD), the Delta D added a major improvement that has become the trademark of Delta launch vehicles.

The Delta D significantly improved payload capacity by incorporating three Castor solid-propellant rocket boosters to "augment" the thrust of the first stage engine.

This strap-on booster configuration was not unique, as it had already been successfully applied to the U.S. Air Force Thrust Augmented Thor-Agena D space launch vehicle.

Although the Thrust Augmented Thor-Agena D was never launched from Cape Canaveral, it preceded the Delta D by about two years.

The three Castor solid rocket boosters were ignited at liftoff, and provided a total thrust of 156,600 pounds. The boosters were jettisoned during flight. An upgraded Rocketdyne first stage engine produced 175,000 pounds of thrust at launch.

The total vehicle could carry a 1,275-pound payload to low-Earth orbit or a 230-pound payload to geostationary transfer orbit.

This effectively doubled the payload capability of the Delta launch vehicle in a period of just four years.

TITAN III-A

Classification: Space Launch Vehicle

Length: 108 feet

Diameter: 10 feet

Date of First Cape Canaveral Launch: September 1, 1964

Date of Final Cape Canaveral Launch: May 6, 1965

Number of Cape Canaveral Launches: 4

The Titan III family of space launch vehicles was born out of a need for rockets capable of carrying payloads heavier than those which could be handled by the Atlas-Centaur.

Introduced in 1964, the Titan III class of rockets was given a numerical designation of SLV-5.

The first of these rockets, the Titan III-A, was basically a Titan II ICBM with an added third stage called a Transtage.

The Transtage employed twin Aerojet engines which burned Aerozine 50/Nitrogen Tetroxide liquid fuel. Each engine could produce an 8,000-pound thrust, giving the Transtage a total thrust of 16,000 pounds.

The overall vehicle could carry a 3,300-pound payload to low-Earth orbit.

The Titan III-A was later modified to carry an Agena third stage in a version introduced as the Titan III-B Agena. The Titan III-B Agena, however, was never launched from Cape Canaveral.

MINUTEMAN II

Classification: Inter-Continental Ballistic Missile

Length: 59 feet, 9 inches

Diameter: 6 feet, 4 inches

Range: 6,990 miles

Date of First Cape Canaveral Launch: September 24, 1964

Date of Final Cape Canaveral Launch: March 14, 1970

Number of Cape Canaveral Launches: 21

Designated LGM-30F Mk II, the Minuteman II represented the second generation of the Minuteman ICBM.

Longer and heavier than the Minuteman I, the Minuteman II could carry 34 percent more propellant, resulting in increased range.

In addition, the Minuteman II carried an improved Aerojet second stage engine. This engine had an increased diameter and submerged exhaust nozzles.

The Minuteman II introduced an Autonetics microelectronic inertial guidance system which could store data on multiple targets. The missile could carry either of two improved versions of Avco re-entry vehicles, each of which could deliver a two-megaton warhead.

In addition, two types of Tracor penaids could be incorporated in the Minuteman II. This was the first time penaids were flown on a U.S. missile.

The first Minuteman II test launch occurred at Cape Canaveral in September, 1964.

The Minuteman II became operational at Grand Forks Air Force Base, North Dakota in 1966. Designated Wing VI, Grand Forks Air Force Base was activated as a Minuteman II base and was the only Minuteman Wing that never deployed the Minuteman I.

Wing VI was structured in an identical fashion to Wings I through IV, with a total of 150 missiles deployed. Eventually, Wing I at Malstrom Air Force Base, Montana was outfitted with an extra 50-missile squadron for the Minuteman II.

This created a maximum deployment capability of 1,000 missiles. With a force made up of a combined Minuteman I and Minuteman II fleet, the full 1,000-missile deployment was achieved by April, 1967.

Following this full deployment, aging Minuteman I missiles were eventually phased out and fully replaced by the Minuteman II and Minuteman III.

DELTA C

Classification: Space Launch Vehicle

Length: 92 feet, 11 inches

Diameter: 8 feet

Date of First Cape Canaveral Launch: October 3, 1964

Date of Final Cape Canaveral Launch: January 22, 1969

Number of Cape Canaveral Launches: 12

Still quite similar to the Delta vehicles which preceded it, the Delta C introduced a modified third stage which improved performance.

The upgraded third stage allowed the Delta C to carry a 900-pound payload to low-Earth orbit or a 180-pound payload to geostationary transfer orbit.

TITAN III-C

Classification: Space Launch Vehicle

Length: 157 feet

Diameter: 10 feet

Date of First Cape Canaveral Launch: June 18, 1965

Date of Final Cape Canaveral Launch: March 6, 1982

Number of Cape Canaveral Launches: 36

An improved version of the Titan III-A, the Titan III-C was introduced in 1965. The most striking modification over the Titan III-A was the addition of two huge strap-on solid rocket boosters.

The United Technologies solid rocket boosters were each 85 feet tall and 10 feet wide and were comprised of five individual segments. Each could produce a remarkable 1,174,600-pound thrust. The boosters burned Powered Aluminum/Ammonium Perchlorate solid fuel.

The Aerojet dual chamber first stage engine could produce a total thrust of 532,000 pounds. An Aerojet second stage engine could produce a 101,000-pound thrust. Both engines burned Aerozine 50/Nitrogen Tetroxide liquid fuel.

The Titan III-C Transtage third stage Aerojet engine also burned Aerozine 50/Nitrogen Tetroxide liquid fuel and could produce a thrust of 16,000 pounds.

With the significant performance improvements which resulted from introducing twin solid rocket boosters, the Titan III-C was able to carry a 29,600-pound payload to low-Earth orbit or a 3,600-pound payload to geostationary transfer orbit.

117

DELTA E

Classification: Space Launch Vehicle

Length: 95 feet, 10 inches

Diameter: 8 feet

Date of First Cape Canaveral Launch: November 6, 1965

Date of Final Cape Canaveral Launch: December 5, 1968

Number of Cape Canaveral Launches: 13

Originally called the Thrust Augmented Improved Delta (TAID), the Delta E featured significant modifications to the previous Delta vehicles to meet specific NASA requirements.

The first stage and three Castor solid rocket boosters operated in an identical fashion to the Delta D.

The second and third stages, however, were redesigned.

The second stage employed an upgraded Aerojet-General engine which produced a thrust of 7,800 pounds for a potential burn time in excess of six minutes. This second stage engine could be re-started in space if necessary.

A completely new United Aircraft solid-propellant third stage motor was introduced and could produce a thrust of 6,000 pounds while reducing the total third stage burn time to 32 seconds.

The total vehicle could carry a 1,600-pound payload to low-Earth orbit or a 330-pound payload to geostationary transfer orbit.

SATURN IB

Classification: Space Launch Vehicle

Length: 224 feet

Diameter: 21 feet, 8 inches

Finspan: 18 feet

Date of First Cape Canaveral Launch: February 26, 1966

Date of Final Cape Canaveral Launch: July 15, 1975

Number of Cape Canaveral Launches: 9

In 1966, the Saturn IB, an improved version of the Saturn I, was brought into service to meet increasing demands of the Apollo program.

Conceived and developed as the Saturn C-IB, the "C" was removed from the name of all Saturn rockets in February, 1963. The Saturn IB was briefly redesignated "Uprated Saturn I" by NASA. However, the name was ultimately changed back to Saturn IB.

Essentially, the Saturn IB was a marriage of an uprated Saturn I first stage to a brand new second stage. The eight Rocketdyne H-1 first stage engines were improved to produce a combined 1,640,000 pounds of thrust at liftoff.

The Saturn IB first stage was designated S-IB. Using a more advanced engine design, Rocketdyne was able to reduce the weight of the H-1 eight-engine array while still improving overall first stage thrust.

The second stage, named S-IVB, marked a significant improvement over the S-IV second stage of the Saturn

I. A single Rocketdyne J-2 engine that powered the S-IVB second stage was capable of producing 225,000 pounds of thrust.

The S-IVB second stage burned liquid oxygen/liquid hydrogen fuel, and was also used as the third stage on the huge Saturn V rockets which would send Apollo astronauts to the Moon.

An advanced stage designed specifically to support manned flight, the S-IVB carried three solid-propellant ullage motors on its aft skirt. These provided positive acceleration for the spacecraft between cutoff and separation of the first stage and ignition of the second stage.

It also carried two auxiliary propulsion system modules located on opposite sides of the aft skirt. These were used for on-orbit spacecraft maneuvering.

A 21-foot, 4-inch ring attached to the top of the S-IVB stage contained an Instrument Unit (IU). Equipment housed in the IU controlled all electronic commands for control and guidance during ascent.

Saturn IB vehicles used for manned flights carried a space capsule and launch escape system. Located at the very top of the rocket, these components were attached to the IU by adapter.

Before Apollo missions were individually numbered, Apollo Saturn IB flights were numbered in series using the numerical designation of each vehicle. The first of these flights was called AS-201.

Each letter and number had a meaning. The "A" stood for Apollo, the "S" stood for Saturn and the "2" indicated that the second generation Saturn vehicle, the Saturn IB, was being flown. The numbers which followed reflected the chronological order of missions.

Thus, "AS-201" meant "Apollo Saturn IB scheduled to be flown as the first in a series of Apollo Saturn IB missions."

The fourth scheduled launch of an Apollo Saturn IB, with a vehicle and mission designation of AS-204, met with tragedy. AS-204 was planned as the first manned flight in the Apollo series. Launch of the 14-day mission had been set for February, 1967.

During a countdown dress rehearsal at Cape Canaveral Launch Complex 34 on January 27, 1967, astronauts Virgil "Gus" Grissom, Ed White and Roger Chaffee were killed when the AS-204 space capsule they occupied caught fire.

Granting honor and respect to the tragedy, NASA later changed the designation of mission AS-204 to Apollo 1. The actual Saturn IB rocket which would have completed Apollo 1 did carry an unmanned Apollo Lunar Module into low-Earth orbit on January 22, 1968.

Following the conclusion of the Apollo lunar program, Saturn IB rockets were used to carry Skylab astronauts into orbit. The Skylab Saturn IB was nearly identical to its Apollo relative, but featured uprated Rocketdyne H-1 engines.

The last Saturn IB flight was conducted in support of the Apollo-Soyuz Test Project (ASTP). AS-210, the ASTP Saturn IB, was eight years old when it carried three astronauts toward their historic rendezvous.

Two unused Saturn IB rockets remained housed in the Vehicle Assembly Building at the Kennedy Space Center following ASTP, which represented the last U.S. manned expendable rocket launch. These Saturn IB rockets were released by NASA for display purposes in December, 1976.

ATLAS-CENTAUR 1966

Classification: Space Launch Vehicle

Length: 131 feet

Diameter: 10 feet

Date of First Cape Canaveral Launch: April 7, 1966

Date of Final Cape Canaveral Launch: July 25, 1990

Number of Cape Canaveral Launches: 63

Introduced in 1966, this improved version of the 1962 Atlas-Centaur featured upgraded Atlas boosters and an improved Centaur second stage to enhance overall vehicle performance.

By this time, it was clear that the operational Atlas missile would soon be eclipsed in the field by more advanced ICBM programs like Titan and Minuteman.

It was also clear that the reliable core vehicle which made up the Atlas ICBM could be refined to fulfill a continuing role as a space launch vehicle even if Atlas missiles were withdrawn from service.

The Atlas-Centaur, as a result, began to develop a life of its own which was no longer directly tied to the Atlas ICBM. For this reason, the 1966 Atlas-Centaur was not simply an Atlas missile with a mated second stage. It was a similar, but independent, class of vehicle.

The new Atlas-Centaur employed two Rocketdyne booster engines with a total thrust of 370,000 pounds. A single Rocketdyne sustainer engine and two Rocketdyne vernier engines provided an additional 61,300 pounds of thrust at liftoff.

An upgraded Centaur second stage, initially designated Centaur D, employed two Pratt and Whitney engines which could produce a combined thrust of 30,000 pounds.

Prior to the next major restructuring of the Atlas-Centaur program in the 1980's, this same basic version of the Atlas-Centaur remained in service, eventually using improved Centaur second stages designated Centaur D1A and Centaur D1AR.

DELTA G

Classification: Space Launch Vehicle

Length: 95 feet, 10 inches

Diameter: 8 feet

Date of First Cape Canaveral Launch: December 14, 1966

Date of Final Cape Canaveral Launch: September 7, 1967

Number of Cape Canaveral Launches: 2

Eliminating the third stage motor, the Delta G was simply an optional two-stage version of the Delta E.

Just two Delta G vehicles were launched from Cape Canaveral. The first carried Biosatellite-1 into low-Earth orbit on December 14, 1966.

The second Delta G launched from the Cape carried Biosatellite-2 into low-Earth orbit on September 7, 1967.

SATURN V APOLLO

Classification: Space Launch Vehicle

Length: 363 feet, 8 inches

Diameter: 33 feet

Finspan: 63 feet

Date of First Cape Canaveral Launch: November 9, 1967

Date of Final Cape Canaveral Launch: December 7, 1972

Number of Cape Canaveral Launches: 12

The world's largest and most powerful space launch vehicle, the Apollo Saturn V was designed and built for the specific purpose of sending men to the Moon.

Design and construction work was initiated under the Saturn C-5 designation in January, 1962. As was the case with the Saturn C-I and Saturn C-IB, the "C" designation was removed in February, 1963.

Although the Saturn V employed some technology which dated back the earliest days of the U.S. space program, the sheer magnitude of the rocket and its mission successfully demonstrated one of the greatest scientific achievements in human history.

One of the legacies of the Saturn V program remains the Kennedy Space Center, which was built on Merritt Island because not enough land was available on Cape Canaveral to support such a large vehicle.

Construction of the most distinctive feature of the Kennedy Space Center, the cavernous Vehicle Assembly Building (VAB), was required to provide a secure indoor facility in which to stack the huge Saturn V components.

Launch Pads 39A and 39B were built, along with numerous Saturn V launch support facilities. The tall Saturn V service gantries were built just outside the VAB.

These were rolled into the VAB atop the Saturn V crawler/transporter, which was adapted from existing Earth-moving machinery. Inside the VAB, the stacked Saturn V was attached to the service structure and both were transported to the launch pad atop the crawler/transporter.

A full test of virgin launch facilities at the Kennedy Space Center was performed on May 25, 1966 using a full-size Saturn V mock-up. The first test launch of a Saturn V occurred from Launch Pad 39A on November 9, 1967. This flight was designated Apollo 4.

A complicated three-stage rocket, the Saturn V employed a total of 41 separate motors to carry the Apollo Command Service Module/Lunar Module (CSM/LM) combination into Earth orbit and lunar trajectory.

The S-IC first stage was built by Boeing and measured 138 feet tall by 33 feet wide with a 63-foot finspan. The powerful first stage employed five Rocketdyne F-1 engines which burned liquid oxygen/RP-1 (kerosene) liquid fuel and produced a combined 7,500,000 pounds of thrust at liftoff.

The S-II second stage was built by North American and measured 81 feet, 6 inches tall by 33 feet wide. It employed five Rocketdyne J-2 engines which burned liquid oxygen/liquid hydrogen and could produce a combined thrust of 1,000,000 pounds.

The S-IVB third stage, also used as a second stage on the Saturn IB, was manufactured by Douglas Aircraft. It measured 58 feet, 8 inches tall by 21 feet, 8 inches wide. The S-IVB employed one Rocketdyne J-2 engine which could produce a thrust of 200,000 pounds.

A NASA-designed and built Instrument Unit (IU) attached to the top of the S-IVB by special adapter measured 3 feet tall by 21 feet, 8 inches wide. The IU housed equipment which controlled all electronic commands for Saturn V control and guidance during ascent.

In a typical Saturn V Apollo flight profile, the five F-1 first stage engines were ignited six seconds before liftoff. The center F-1 engine was shut down 135 seconds after launch. The outer four F-1 engines were shut down 15 seconds later.

One second following cutoff of the four outer F-1 engines, the first stage separated. Simultaneously, eight retro-rockets were fired for less than one second to slow the forward speed of the first stage, thus keeping it from bumping into the second stage.

These first stage retro-rockets were located in pairs at the base of each of the outer four F-1 engines. They provided a total thrust of 88,500 pounds. Following separation, the spent first stage fell back into the Atlantic Ocean about 400 miles downrange.

One second after first stage separation, eight solid-fueled motors mounted on the first/second stage adapter ring were fired for four seconds. These provided a combined thrust of 181,000 pounds.

In addition to maintaining the positive motion of the rocket, these motors performed an ullage maneuver, forcing the second stage fuel to the bottom of its tanks in order to feed the engines. The five J-2 second stage engines were fired during this ullage burn.

Thirty seconds following second stage ignition, the first/second stage adapter ring separated and slid past the second stage engines for a tumble back toward Earth. Six seconds following this, the Apollo spacecraft escape tower was jettisoned.

The second stage engines burned for 365 seconds prior to separation from the third stage. At separation, four solid-fueled second stage retro-rockets were fired to keep the second and third stages from hitting one another.

These four retro-rockets were located in a conical adapter on the front face of the second stage. They provided a total thrust of 140,000 pounds. The second stage began its tumble, eventually impacting the Atlantic Ocean about 2,500 miles downrange.

At this point, the Saturn V had achieved a speed of 15,700 m.p.h. and an altitude of 115 miles.

Two solid-fueled ullage motors located 180 degrees apart on the third stage aft skirt were fired for four seconds to settle the liquid fuel. These motors produced 6,800 pounds of thrust.

Three seconds after second stage separation, the S-IVB third stage J-2 engine was ignited. Nine seconds later, the third stage ullage motors which fired at separation and their cases were jettisoned.

The third stage J-2 engine was fired for 142 seconds before being shut down. This initial S-IVB burn was sufficient to carry the Apollo spacecraft into a 118-mile orbit at a speed of 17,500 m.p.h.

At the end of this first S-IVB burn, two ullage motors were fired to settle the remaining fuel and provide spacecraft stabilization. These ullage motors were housed in two Auxiliary Propulsion System (APS) modules located 80 degrees apart on the third stage aft skirt.

Each APS module housed three attitude control motors and one ullage motor. The attitude control motors could each produce 150 pounds of thrust, while the ullage motors could each produce 70 pounds of thrust. All burned nitrogen tetroxide/hydrazine liquid fuel.

During two or three checkout orbits, the S-IVB attitude control motors could be fired in sequence to make any necessary on-orbit corrections. Following these checkout orbits, the ullage motors were fired for 77 seconds to settle the fuel and provide forward spacecraft momentum.

The third stage J-2 engine was then re-ignited for 345 seconds to achieve a speed of 25,000 m.p.h.. This second J-2 firing was necessary to carry the Apollo spacecraft out of Earth orbit and place it on a proper trajectory toward the Moon.

Once the Apollo spacecraft was on its way to the Moon, the Saturn V had completed its job. The S-IVB third stage separated from the Apollo CSM/LM combination. The third stage ullage motors were fired for 280 seconds to move the S-IVB away from the CSM/LM.

The third stage J-2 engine was then fired for the last time until its remaining fuel was spent. Depending upon the specific Apollo mission profile, the S-IVB was either sent toward deep space or the Moon.

In several instances, spent S-IVB stages actually hit the Moon, with the resulting impact being measured by seismometers placed on the lunar surface by the Apollo astronauts.

Although a two-stage version of the Saturn V was used to carry the Skylab space station into orbit, the huge rocket was effectively retired at the conclusion of the Apollo program.

During its development, the Saturn V was considered as a workhorse booster of a planned Apollo Applications space science program which would follow the lunar landing missions.

The Apollo Applications program never materialized as NASA chose instead to develop the Space Shuttle. In December, 1976, NASA released components of two remaining vehicles along with test articles which eventually facilitated the completion of three Saturn V displays.

MINUTEMAN III

Classification: Inter-Continental Ballistic Missile

Length: 59 feet, 9 inches

Diameter: 6 feet, 4 inches

Range: 8,078 miles

Date of First Cape Canaveral Launch: August 16, 1968

Date of Final Cape Canaveral Launch: December 14, 1970

Number of Cape Canaveral Launches: 17

The Minuteman III, designated LGM-30G Mk III, completed the evolution of the Minuteman family by introducing a new third stage and advanced re-entry vehicle.

Aerojet and Thiokol jointly designed the third stage engine, which could produce a thrust of 34,400 pounds. The engine employed a single fluid injection nozzle.

The third stage also featured a new post-boost propulsion system from Bell Aerospace. The advanced system increased guidance accuracy by employing a 300-pound thrust motor for forward motion, a 22-pound thrust motor for pitch/yaw and an 18-pound thrust motor for roll.

A dramatically improved GE re-entry vehicle was itself made up of three separate, maneuverable re-entry vehicles. Each re-entry vehicle could be independently targeted and could carry a 200 kiloton warhead.

Warhead capacity was later increased to 350 kilotons with the introduction of a further upgraded GE re-entry vehicle.

The total package had a total circular target error of just 1,200 feet at a range of over 8,000 miles.

By February, 1969, all LGM-30A Minuteman I missiles had been withdrawn from service, leaving a 1,000-Minuteman force with a combination of LGM-30B Minuteman I and Minuteman II missiles.

The first Minuteman III squadron was activated at Minot Air Force Base, North Dakota (Wing III) in December, 1970.

Full force modernization of the Minuteman Wings had begun, and by July, 1975, all remaining LGM-30B Minuteman I missiles had been removed from service.

The ultimate deployment was made up of a mixed fleet of Minuteman II and Minuteman III missiles deployed at all six operational wings.

As per the original plans, 200 missiles each were deployed at Wings I and V, while 150 missiles each were deployed at Wings II, III, IV and VI, comprising a total force of 1,000.

At its peak, the Minuteman fleet had a standing capability of delivering 2,100 warheads. In addition, a technical option was left open to carry satellites aboard Minuteman III silo-based missiles.

Although this was never actually done, the U.S. Air Force proposed this option in case launch sites at Vandenberg Air Force Base, California or Cape Canaveral became disabled by acts of war.

Indeed, feasibility studies are currently underway to determine if retired Minuteman III missiles can be modified to carry satellites, although new above-ground launch facilities would need to be constructed first.

POSEIDON

Classification: Fleet Ballistic Missile

Note: Fleet Ballistic Missiles are also referred to as Submarine-Launched Ballistic Missiles.

Length: 34 feet

Diameter: 6 feet, 2 inches

Range: 2,880 miles

Date of First Cape Canaveral Launch: August 16, 1968

Date of Final Cape Canaveral Launch: April 30, 1990

Number of Cape Canaveral Launches: 268

Originally called the Polaris B3, the Poseidon C3 was granted a new name due to some significant technical advances over its Polaris ancestors.

Designated UGM-73A, it is acceptable to refer to the Poseidon C3 simply as Poseidon, because unlike the Polaris, only one version of the Poseidon was ever deployed.

Tests between 1960 and 1962 determined that glass-fiber liners and locating rings which surrounded the Polaris missiles as they sat in their launch tubes could be safely removed without adversely affecting a missile's operation.

As a result, missiles with a larger width could be safely housed in the same launch tubes used for the narrower Polaris. This allowed the U.S. Navy to deploy a larger, improved Fleet Ballistic Missile (FBM) without having to make major modifications to existing launch tubes.

In addition to being wider than its Polaris relatives, the Poseidon sported a completely new guidance system managed by MIT and built by GE, Hughes and Raytheon. The inertial guidance system was tied to a GE fire control system.

Trajectory data was updated continuously by an Autonetics and Sperry Ship's Inertial Navigation System as the submarine's position changed. All Poseidon guidance components employed digital microelectronics technology.

The gas pressure necessary to force the tightly fitting Poseidon out of its launch tube was produced by steam generated from a solid-fueled water boiler. Under operational conditions, one Poseidon missile could be launched every 50 seconds.

The Poseidon first stage employed a Thiokol/Hercules solid-fueled engine, while the second stage employed a Hercules solid-fueled engine. Both stages were contained in glass filament-wound casings, and each was maneuvered by a single gimbaled exhaust nozzle.

Each Lockheed/AEC Poseidon warhead contained a total of ten independently targeted re-entry vehicles, each of which had a 50-kiloton capability.

The warhead could be adapted to contain a total of 14 re-entry vehicles, but this configuration reduced the missile's range to that of the Polaris A3. For this reason, the array utilizing ten re-entry vehicles per warhead was preferred for deployment.

The first Poseidon test launch occurred on August 16, 1968. The first submarine-based test launch occurred on August 3, 1970 from SSBN 627 James Madison. The Poseidon was declared operational on March 31, 1971 and was deployed aboard all 31 Lafayette Class submarines.

In 1973, Poseidon test launches uncovered some operational flaws in the missile which required a modification program to correct. Poseidon submarines already deployed had their missiles modified upon returning to port. New submarines received an improved Poseidon upon deployment.

DELTA M

Classification: Space Launch Vehicle

Length: 106 feet, 4 inches

Diameter: 8 feet

Date of First Cape Canaveral Launch: September 18, 1968

Date of Final Cape Canaveral Launch: February 2, 1971

Number of Cape Canaveral Launches: 12

Like the Delta L, the Delta M was referred to as a Long Tank Delta (LTD) or Long Tank Thrust Augmented Delta (LTTAD).

However, the Delta M was a Delta J with an elongated first stage fuel tank and improved Castor solid rocket boosters.

Stated more simply, the Delta L and Delta M were identical except for the third stage. The Delta L carried the Delta E third stage, while the Delta M carried the Delta J third stage.

The Delta M could carry a 2,200-pound payload to low-Earth orbit or a 785-pound payload to geostationary transfer orbit.

DELTA N

Classification: Space Launch Vehicle

Length: 106 feet, 4 inches

Diameter: 8 feet

Date of First Cape Canaveral Launch: February 26, 1969

Date of Final Cape Canaveral Launch: September 29, 1971

Number of Cape Canaveral Launches: 4

Delta N was the designation given to the optional two-stage version of either the Delta L or Delta M.

Since the Delta L and Delta M were identical with the exception of the third stage, the Delta N did not require more than one numerical designation.

It was simply a Delta L or Delta M first and second stage combination with the third stage eliminated.

DELTA L

Classification: Space Launch Vehicle

Length: 106 feet, 4 inches

Diameter: 8 feet

Date of First Cape Canaveral Launch: August 27, 1969

Date of Final Cape Canaveral Launch: August 27, 1969

Number of Cape Canaveral Launches: 1

Alternately referred to as a Long Tank Delta (LTD) or Long Tank Thrust Augmented Delta (LTTAD), the Delta L was essentially a Delta E with an elongated first stage fuel tank and improved Castor solid rocket boosters.

DELTA M-6

Classification: Space Launch Vehicle

Length: 106 feet, 4 inches

Diameter: 8 feet

Date of First Cape Canaveral Launch: March 13, 1971

Date of Final Cape Canaveral Launch: March 13, 1971

Number of Cape Canaveral Launches: 1

Nearly identical to the Delta M, the Delta M-6 added three Castor solid rocket boosters, for a total of six.

Three solid rocket boosters were ignited at liftoff, while three were ignited 31 seconds later to lengthen the overall period that the boosters contributed to the vehicle's overall thrust.

The additional three solid rocket boosters allowed the Delta M-6 to carry a 2,900-pound payload to low-Earth orbit or a 1,000-pound payload to geostationary transfer orbit. This represented a nearly five-fold increase in the Delta launch vehicle's payload capability during its first decade of operation.

An optional two-stage version of the Delta M-6 was introduced as the Delta N-6, but the Delta N-6 was never launched from Cape Canaveral.

DELTA 1000 SERIES

Classification: Space Launch Vehicle

Length: 106 feet, 4 inches

Diameter: 8 feet

Date of First Cape Canaveral Launch: September 22, 1972

Date of Final Cape Canaveral Launch: June 21, 1975

Number of Cape Canaveral Launches: 6

In order to describe the Delta 1000 Series rockets, it is first necessary to provide a description of an interim version of the Delta introduced as the Delta 900 Series.

Delta 900 Series rockets were never launched from Cape Canaveral, but the vehicle did introduce enhancements which proved to be significant in Delta rocket evolution.

A description of the Delta 1000 Series rockets, which were launched from Cape Canaveral, follows the description of the Delta 900 Series.

DELTA 900 SERIES

Classification: Space Launch Vehicle

Length: 106 feet, 4 inches

Diameter: 8 feet

Although Delta 900 Series rockets were never launched from Cape Canaveral, the introduction of the vehicle marked an important step in the evolution of the Delta program, and a vital link to the Delta rockets which followed.

The Delta 900 Series launch vehicle added three Castor II solid rocket boosters to a cluster of six already employed for a total of nine. The rocket also introduced improved guidance and electronics.

The second stage featured an improved Aerojet-General engine which burned Aerozine 50/nitrogen tetroxide liquid fuel, providing a thrust of 9,800 pounds.

Six of the nine solid rocket boosters were ignited at liftoff. These burned out and were jettisoned as the remaining three were ignited and burned for an additional 39 seconds.

The nine solid rocket boosters contributed a total of 480,600 pounds of thrust to the overall vehicle.

The two-stage Delta 900 Series rocket, designated Delta 900, could carry a 3,700-pound payload to low-Earth orbit.

The three-stage version, designated Delta 904, could carry a 1,400-pound payload to geostationary transfer orbit.

DELTA 1000 SERIES

Looking quite similar to the modern Delta launch vehicle, the Delta 1000 Series introduced an extended long tank configuration which has come to be known as "straight-eight".

While previous Delta rockets were tapered at the top, the Delta 1000 Series vehicles extended the 8-foot first stage diameter all the way to the top, with the exception of the rounded conical tip of the payload fairing.

Since the upper stage diameters were now the same as the first stage, additional room was available at the top of the rocket to handle larger payloads.

This upward extension of the first stage wall also provided added structural support for heavier payloads.

Otherwise identical to the Delta 900 Series vehicle, the Delta 1000 Series offered an optional solid-propellant third stage which could produce a thrust of 15,400 pounds.

This additional modification allowed the three-stage version of the Delta 1000 Series rocket to carry a 1,500-pound payload to geostationary transfer orbit.

The "straight-eight" structural modification alone allowed the two-stage version of the Delta 1000 Series rocket to carry a 4,000-pound payload to low-Earth orbit.

PERSHING IA

Classification: Medium-Range Ballistic Missile

Length: 34 feet, 10 inches

Diameter: 3 feet, 4 inches

Finspan: 5 feet, 9 inches

Range: 460 miles

Date of First Cape Canaveral Launch: February 21, 1973

Date of Final Cape Canaveral Launch: October 13, 1983

Number of Cape Canaveral Launches: 100

In 1967, production of the Pershing I was switched to the Pershing IA. The Pershing IA was essentially the same missile matched to a more streamlined set of support vehicles.

The primary improvement was the inclusion of the missile and its warhead in the same vehicle. In addition, the Pershing IA and its support vehicles could be transported aboard U.S. Air Force C-130 aircraft, which improved the speed and efficiency of deployment.

The Pershing IA remained unchanged until 1976, when European-based missiles were equipped with an Automatic Azimuth Reference System and Sequential Launch Adapter.

These devices allowed one field commander to automatically launch three missiles in sequence. Launches could be conducted with only a brief delay, even from previously unsurveyed launch sites.

Pershing IA production ceased in 1971 with the development of the vastly improved Pershing II.

SATURN V SKYLAB

Classification: Space Launch Vehicle

Length: 333 feet, 8 inches

Diameter: 33 feet

Finspan: 63 feet

Date of First Cape Canaveral Launch: May 14, 1973

Date of Final Cape Canaveral Launch: May 14, 1973

Number of Cape Canaveral Launches: 1

The Skylab Saturn V was a two-stage version of the Apollo Saturn V adapted for the specific purpose of carrying the Skylab space station into low-Earth orbit. Both the S-IC first stage and S-II second stage were improved to support the Skylab launch.

The five Rocketdyne F-1 first stage engines were uprated to produce a total thrust of 7,723,726 pounds at lift-off. The five Rocketdyne J-2 second stage engines were uprated to produce a total thrust of 1,125,000 pounds.

DELTA 2000 SERIES

Classification: Space Launch Vehicle

Length: 116 feet

Diameter: 8 feet

Date of First Cape Canaveral Launch: January 18, 1974

Date of Final Cape Canaveral Launch: August 9, 1979

Number of Cape Canaveral Launches: 34

The Delta 2000 Series launch vehicle incorporated several major improvements to earlier Delta rockets.

The same Castor solid rocket boosters used in the Delta 900 and 1000 Series vehicles were employed in the Delta 2000 Series. The first and second stages, however, were completely upgraded.

A more powerful Rocketdyne first stage engine, adapted from the H-1 Saturn I and Saturn IB first stage engines, could produce a thrust of 205,000 pounds at liftoff.

A TRW second stage engine, adapted from the Apollo Lunar Module, provided 9,400 pounds of thrust. The second stage engine was fed by Aerozine-50/nitrogen tetroxide liquid fuel.

Capable of carrying a maximum 4,400-pound payload to low-Earth orbit or a 1,593-pound payload to geostationary transfer orbit, Delta 2000 Series vehicles could be delivered in a variety of configurations to meet specific needs.

Options included two or three stages, as well as three, four, six or nine solid rocket boosters.

The Delta 2000 Series was, at the time, regarded by NASA as the last generation Delta that would be necessary to meet existing needs.

However, the Delta continued to evolve as commercial satellite manufacturers needed a launch vehicle capable of carrying payloads too heavy for the Delta 2000 Series but not heavy enough to justify the use of an Atlas-Centaur.

Certainly, incorporating modifications to the existing Delta family would fill this gap in payload capability much more efficiently than creating an entirely new class of launch vehicle.

TITAN III-E CENTAUR

Classification: Space Launch Vehicle

Length: 160 feet, 1 inch

Diameter: 10 feet

Date of First Cape Canaveral Launch: February 11, 1974

Date of Final Cape Canaveral Launch: September 5, 1977

Number of Cape Canaveral Launches: 7

A modified version of the U.S. Air Force Titan III-D, the Titan III-E Centaur was introduced in 1974 to meet the launch requirements for a number of NASA scientific payloads.

While the Titan III-D was a two-stage rocket, the Titan III-E Centaur featured the addition of a Centaur D-1T third stage.

The Centaur D-1T was powered by two Pratt and Whitney engines which burned liquid oxygen/liquid hydrogen liquid fuel and could produce a combined thrust of 30,000 pounds.

Two United Technologies solid rocket boosters burned Powered Aluminum/Ammonium Perchlorate solid fuel and produced a combined thrust of 2,361,000 pounds.

The first stage Aerojet dual-chamber first stage engine could produce a 530,000-pound thrust. An Aerojet second stage engine was capable of producing a thrust of 101,000 pounds. The first and second stage engines both burned Aerozine 50/Nitrogen Tetroxide liquid fuel.

The overall vehicle was able to carry a 7,400-pound payload to geostationary transfer orbit, an 8,400-pound payload to a Mars or Venus trajectory or a 500 to 1,750-pound payload on a trajectory to the outer planets.

SRAM

Classification: Air-to-Surface Cruise Missile

Length: 15 feet, 10 inches (with tail fairing)

Length: 14 feet (without tail fairing)

Diameter: 18 inches

Finspan: 15 inches

Range: 105 miles

Date of First Cape Canaveral Launch: August 20, 1974

Date of Final Cape Canaveral Launch: July 26, 1983

Number of Cape Canaveral Launches: 31

The SRAM, or "Short Range Attack Missile", was proposed in 1960. The reduction in the size and weight of nuclear payloads made the development of this small, lightweight aircraft-deployed missile feasible.

Designed to be carried aboard Strategic Air Command (SAC) aircraft, the SRAM was intended to carry small but potent nuclear weapons a distance of about 100 miles.

The missile would primarily be deployed to destroy or neutralize enemy defenses such as radar sites, missile bases and air bases. Since the SRAM was relatively small, as many as 44 missiles could be carried on a single aircraft.

This vastly increased the number of targets that one aircraft could attack during a single engagement.

Boeing was selected by the U.S. Air Force to begin SRAM feasibility studies in December, 1963. At this time, the SRAM was classified under Weapons System-140A (WS-140A).

In October, 1966, Boeing was awarded a production contract for the SRAM, now designated AGM-69A. A dummy prototype of the SRAM was first dropped from an aircraft in December, 1967.

Live test flights of the SRAM commenced in 1969. The SRAM was declared operational by early 1972. Boeing completed a production run of 1,500 missiles by July, 1975.

Carried aboard B-52G, B-52H and FB-111A aircraft, SRAM missiles were flown out of a total of 18 SAC bases.

Inertial guidance of the SRAM was provided by a Singer-Kearfott system, with a Delco on-board computer allowing four different flight profiles for each missile.

The SRAM was quite hard to detect by enemy radar because of its small, streamlined size. In fact, the missile in flight was as hard to detect as a bullet.

Each B-52 aircraft could carry eight SRAM missiles on a rotary launch "revolver" cylinder carried in the aft bomb bay. In some instances, up to three more identical cylinders could be carried internally. This array provided a maximum of 32 missiles, excluding wing deployment.

Pylons located under each B-52 wing were first built for Hound Dog missiles. These pylons, one under each wing, were modified to carry six SRAM each. The pylons thus accommodated a total of 12 missiles, creating a maximum SRAM capability of 44 missiles per each B-52.

Each FB-111A aircraft could carry a maximum of six SRAM. Four missiles were located on swiveling wing pylons, while two missiles could be carried internally.

A Lockheed two-pulse solid rocket motor fired the SRAM to a maximum speed of Mach 3. Each SRAM carried a warhead with the capability of delivering a maximum 200-kiloton nuclear payload.

U.S. Air Force plans to develop an improved SRAM designated AGM-69B were scrapped in 1976. Instead, a decision was made to periodically upgrade the existing SRAM fleet as technology advancements were made available.

DELTA 3000 SERIES

Classification: Space Launch Vehicle

Length: 116 feet

Diameter: 8 feet

Date of First Cape Canaveral Launch: December 12, 1975

Date of Final Cape Canaveral Launch: March 24, 1989

Number of Cape Canaveral Launches: 33

The Delta 3000 Series was born out of the need for a rocket capable of carrying payloads too heavy for the Delta 2000 Series but not heavy enough to require the use of an Atlas-Centaur.

Since NASA did not envision a need for a new medium-weight launch vehicle so close to the introduction of their Space Shuttle, the space agency was reluctant to provide financing for this next generation Delta rocket.

However, NASA was able to provide a blessing for the vehicle, if not backed by up-front money.

NASA did envision a use for the Delta 3000 Series as an interim launch vehicle to handle medium-weight payloads prior to operational flights of the Space Shuttle, which at the time were nearly a decade away.

As a result, McDonnell Douglas was able to secure private industrial financing for the introduction of the Delta 3000 Series. NASA provided no research and development funding, but did purchase the completed vehicles in support of civilian and commercial satellite launches.

Although similar in basic design to the Delta 2000 Series, the Delta 3000 Series introduced larger, more powerful Castor solid rocket boosters.

The improved solid rocket boosters were 36 feet, 5 inches tall and 3 feet, 4 inches wide, and could each produce a thrust of 84,000 pounds.

The total package of nine improved solid rocket boosters increased the overall Delta 3000 Series vehicle thrust about 100,000 pounds over that of the comparable Delta 2000 Series rocket.

Typically, five of the nine solid rocket boosters were ignited at liftoff. Along with the Rocketdyne first stage engine, a total thrust of 630,600 pounds was produced at launch.

The remaining four solid rocket boosters were ignited following burnout and jettison of the first five.

In its original configuration, the three-stage Delta 3000 Series vehicle was capable of carrying a 2,100-pound payload to geostationary transfer orbit.

A Payload Assist Module (PAM) was offered as an optional third stage in the Delta 3000 Series. The Thiokol PAM third stage motor, with a thrust of 13,000 pounds, allowed the total vehicle to carry a 2,300-pound payload to geostationary transfer orbit.

This represented almost a 50 percent increase in payload capability over the Delta 2000 Series.

An improved PAM, called PAM-D, was later introduced. It further increased the Delta 3000 Series payload capacity.

Using the PAM-D third stage, the total vehicle was capable of carrying a 2,800-pound payload into geostationary transfer orbit.

TRIDENT I

Classification: Fleet Ballistic Missile

Note: Fleet Ballistic Missiles are also referred to as Submarine-Launched Ballistic Missiles.

Length: 34 feet

Diameter: 6 feet, 2 inches

Range: 4,350 miles

Date of First Cape Canaveral Launch: January 18, 1977

Date of Final Cape Canaveral Launch: December 18, 2001

Number of Cape Canaveral Launches: 162

The Trident project was initiated in 1972 to provide a more effective missile than the Poseidon for the U.S. Navy Undersea Long-Range Missile System (ULMS).

Originally called "Expo" for "Extended-Range Poseidon", the Trident I C4 was based upon the Poseidon missile and was designed to be retrofitted to existing Poseidon submarines.

As was the case with the Poseidon C3, which is acceptably referred to as Poseidon, the Trident I C4 may be accurately referred to simply as Trident I because only one version of the missile was ever deployed.

The Trident I was basically a Poseidon missile with an added third stage and several technical modifications.

Although it was designed to be launched in the same fashion as the Poseidon, the Trident I employed an aerospike, or long pointed probe, which extended from the missile's nose upon first stage ignition.

The aerospike was designed to create an inclined shockwave during flight, which resulted in less stress on the missile as well as improved aerodynamic efficiency.

The Trident I also added a post-boost propulsion system to help guide the weapons payload to its target. A stellar sensor was incorporated during the post-boost phase to monitor final trajectory.

With Lockheed as its prime contractor, the Trident I carried a solid-fueled Thiokol first stage, Hercules second stage and UTC/CSD third stage.

Although deployment of the Trident I was extended due to budget problems and certain technical challenges, the missile was declared operational in September, 1982.

In addition to being deployed aboard retrofitted Lafayette class submarines, the Trident I precipitated the introduction of a new breed of Fleet Ballistic Missile (FBM) submarines known as the Ohio class.

Ohio class submarines incorporate advanced sonar and communications capabilities and can carry up to 24 missiles each, compared to 16 missiles each for the Lafayette class.

CHEVALINE

Classification: Fleet Ballistic Missile

Note: Fleet Ballistic Missiles are also referred to as Submarine-Launched Ballistic Missiles

Length: 32 feet, 4 inches

Diameter: 4 feet, 6 inches

Range: 2,880 miles

Date of First Cape Canaveral Launch: September 12, 1977

Date of Final Cape Canaveral Launch: May 10, 1987

Number of Cape Canaveral Launches: 34

Chevaline is the British designation for a fleet of Polaris A3 missiles sold to Great Britain by the United States and styled for deployment on British submarines. Other than the fact that Chevaline is a British weapons program, Chevaline missiles are identical to the Polaris A3.

Chevaline missiles underwent a variety of remanufacture and upgrades prior to being withdrawn from service in the mid 1980's.

SPACE SHUTTLE

Length: 122 feet, 2 inches

Height: 56 feet, 8 inches

Diameter: 22 feet, 8 inches

Wingspan: 78 feet, 1 inch

Date of First Launch: April 12, 1981

Date of Final Launch: July 8, 2011

Number of Launches: 135

Born in 1968 at the height of the Apollo program, the Space Shuttle was designed to fulfill two basic roles in NASA post-Apollo manned flight objectives.

The first goal of the Space Shuttle program was to provide NASA with an efficient, re-usable method of carrying astronauts to and from a permanently manned space station.

At the time, NASA envisioned a space station which would be staffed by 12 to 24 people. The space station was intended to assure a permanent manned U.S. presence in space following the Apollo lunar landings.

The space station would support a plethora of scientific research objectives, plus act as an engineering and support base for manned journeys to the planets.

In addition, NASA believed that Space Shuttles could serve as multi-purpose satellite delivery vehicles with the potential to completely replace Atlas-Centaur, Delta and Titan rockets.

The words "cheap" and "routine" were the words which most closely matched the objectives for Space Shuttles as expressed by NASA. Of course, history would prove otherwise.

On January 31, 1969, NASA issued feasibility design study contracts for their "Integrated Launch and Re-entry Vehicle" (ILRV). Invitations were given to four aerospace contractors to present design proposals on re-usable and partially re-usable manned spacecraft.

These companies presented reports to NASA by November 1, 1969. They unanimously recommended a fully re-usable, two-stage vehicle.

Early in 1970, NASA refined their technical requirements for the vehicle. The name "Space Shuttle" first appeared in the "purpose" section of an official invitation for production contract bids issued on February 18, 1970.

The name "Space Shuttle" subsequently became a permanent fixture for the vehicle, which NASA agreed should incorporate a fully re-usable, two-stage design.

With great optimism, NASA initially expected that the first Space Shuttle would enter service by 1977. In 1971, North American Rockwell and McDonnell Douglas were granted production contracts.

From that point on, development of the Space Shuttle became extremely complicated, with the future of the vehicle often in doubt from one year to the next.

At first, doubts surfaced about the feasibility of developing a two-stage Space Shuttle. To analyze these concerns, NASA issued study contracts to Grumman/Boeing, Lockheed and Chrysler in June, 1971.

In basic terms, the initial NASA concept for the two-stage Space Shuttle called for a smaller manned winged vehicle to sit atop a larger manned winged vehicle. These would be pad-launched from a vertical position.

The larger winged vehicle would be called the "Booster", while the smaller winged vehicle would be called the "Orbiter". The Booster would carry the Orbiter to an altitude of about 50 miles. The Orbiter would then separate and fire its own engines to reach orbit.

After separation, the Booster would turn and descend through the atmosphere for a landing near the launch site. The Orbiter would return for a landing upon the conclusion of its space mission.

The Booster would, in essence, be a fuel tank with wings. In this two-stage concept, both the Booster and Orbiter would require cockpits, hardware and instrumentation to facilitate landings.

Both were designed to carry internal turbo-fan engines which would produce controlled flight during landing operations. Each vehicle would carry its own fuel tanks.

As originally described by NASA in 1970, this two-stage Space Shuttle would be able to carry a 25,000-pound payload to a maximum 300-mile circular orbit.

As we now know, this early two-stage concept obviously does not resemble the Space Shuttles which were eventually built. This was due to the economic realities facing NASA in the early 1970's.

In a time of general recession, it was clear that NASA could not afford to build a fleet of complicated two-stage Space Shuttles along with a space station at the same time. Utilizing the intent of the day for the Space Shuttle, one without the other made no sense at all.

Matters were further complicated in 1971 as NASA negotiated with the U.S. Air Force regarding shared use of the Space Shuttle fleet. Military funding for the Space Shuttle program was vital if NASA hoped to build the vehicle at all.

But the U.S. Air Force specified a total payload capability of 65,000 pounds for Space Shuttles capable of carrying large, sophisticated military satellites into orbit. This figure was nearly three times more than NASA had originally planned.

These major factors led to a dramatic redesign of the Space Shuttle and the proposed space station.

The NASA space station was originally designed following the Skylab pattern. A single multi-deck structure which made up the space station would be carried into orbit by a Saturn V rocket. Space Shuttles would then only be needed to ferry astronauts, equipment and supplies.

It was thought that this type of space station would have a useful life of about ten years, at which time it could simply be replaced by another. However, an "all at once" space station did not fit the NASA budget.

NASA decided to adopt a modular concept for the space station. The space station would be built piece by piece over a period of years, with separate modules carried into orbit by Space Shuttles.

This was a prudent move for NASA. Not only did it provide a more realistic approach for constructing a space station, it also made possible the production of a redesigned Space Shuttle capable of carrying heavy military payloads and even commercial satellites.

In redesigning the Space Shuttle as a space station module carrier, U.S. Air Force payload criteria were met, thus assuring critical military funding. Just as important, the redesign would allow NASA to carry a plethora of satellites aboard Space Shuttles.

Over time, this could produce tremendous cost savings for NASA. Not only could NASA secure private funding to carry commercial satellites aboard Space Shuttles, the costs of maintaining Atlas-Centaur, Delta and Titan rocket fleets could be phased out and ultimately eliminated.

With an event like the Challenger explosion never anticipated, NASA made a decision, so to speak, to "put all of their eggs in one basket". The Space Shuttle was to be a multi-purpose manned vehicle which would carry NASA into the next century.

Even with major design modifications, NASA faced a huge price tag for its Space Shuttle fleet. On July 1, 1971, NASA granted four-month contract extensions to Rockwell and McDonnell Douglas to come up with methods of cutting their projected $10 billion development costs.

The contractors decided that the most suitable method of cutting costs was to scrap the manned Booster stage of the Space Shuttle. NASA opted instead to create a more traditional expendable system to carry the manned Orbiter into space.

NASA kept the manned Booster on the drawing boards, though, in case it could be afforded at a later date. Reduction in the overall size and complexity of the Space Shuttle booster system and redesign of the Orbiter did provide cost savings, but additional changes were ahead.

A smaller version of the Orbiter, called Mark I, was planned initially. This could later be replaced by a larger Mark II version of the Orbiter. The development of the Mark I and Mark II Space Shuttle fleet was to be phased in over a period of several years.

The Orbiter itself could be scaled down considerably as NASA agreed to use external fuel tanks to carry the fuel the spacecraft would need to reach orbit. In previous designs, the Orbiter would carry its own fuel tanks on board.

In September, 1971, Boeing proposed using a modified S-IC first stage from the Saturn V to act as a main fuel tank for the Space Shuttle. In one version, the S-IC could be equipped with a crew compartment, wings and aerodynamic equipment to facilitate a manned Booster landing.

The "Re-usable S-IC" Booster, called RS-IC, would carry the Orbiter aloft. Following separation, the Orbiter would reach orbit powered by its own engines, fed by two external liquid hydrogen tanks which would be jettisoned in space. The RS-IC would then return for a landing.

A more cost-effective version involved using a modified S-IC Saturn V first stage as an unmanned Booster which would be attached to a large external fuel tank. This array would be mated to the Orbiter.

The S-IC would then act as an expendable Booster which would separate at an altitude of about 45 miles, leaving the Orbiter to reach orbit using its own engines fueled by the remaining single external fuel tank which would be jettisoned in space.

With the exception of the S-IC booster, this design was somewhat similar to the vehicles which eventually flew. The S-IC option was scrapped because the booster burned liquid oxygen and kerosene. This fuel combination was deemed too inefficient for the Space Shuttle.

Space Shuttle development contracts for Rockwell, Grumman/Boeing and Lockheed were extended through February, 1972, and two core concepts for the spacecraft emerged. These were divided into parallel burn and series burn concepts.

In the parallel burn concept, the Orbiter's engines ignited at the same time as the Booster. The Orbiter's engines would fire all the way to orbit, which would require them to be fed by a large external fuel tank.

The Booster system would be jettisoned at some point during ascent. Initial options for the Booster called for various combinations of large or medium-sized solid rocket boosters with the possibility of high-pressure liquid fuel assist.

One popular parallel burn Booster combination called for two large solid rocket boosters to be assisted by four smaller solid rocket boosters which would be strapped to the Orbiter's large external fuel tank.

In the series burn concept, or multi-stage approach, the Orbiter's engines would still be fed by an external fuel tank. However, the Orbiter's engines would not fire until a first stage Booster had first been expended in flight.

Series burn first stage arrays on the drawing board for the Space Shuttle called for various combinations of clustered solid rocket boosters, clustered modified Saturn V F-1 engines or new high-pressure liquid fueled engines.

NASA again encountered development difficulties because all of the parallel and series burn concepts presented proved to be too expensive to be manufactured under tight budgetary constraints.

A company named Mathematica was retained by NASA to perform an economic analysis of the entire Space Shuttle program. The company would recommend the most cost-effective design for the vehicle, as well as tally funding alternatives such as commercial launch revenue.

Mathematica did provide some encouragement at a critical time for NASA. It was almost immediately determined that the U.S. manned space program would be more cost-effectively served by Space Shuttles rather than continued use of expendable rockets like Saturn IB and Saturn V.

The federal Office of Management and Budget (OMB) scrutinized NASA expenditures and the agency's proposals for the Space Shuttle. Initial reactions of OMB to the Space Shuttle were not encouraging, so NASA took its case directly to President Richard M. Nixon.

Late in 1971, there was a chance that the Space Shuttle program would be halted for more than one year. NASA had no guarantee that President Nixon would recommend any expenditures for the Space Shuttle in his fiscal year 1973 budget, which ran from July 1, 1972 to June 30, 1973.

President Nixon was ready to present his fiscal year 1973 budget to the U.S. Congress in early January, 1972. If he did not endorse funds for the Space Shuttle in this budget, the program could have faced a stall until July, 1973 at the earliest.

NASA Administrator James Fletcher and NASA Deputy Administrator George Low met with President Nixon for 45 minutes at the "San Clemente White House" on January 5, 1972. A decision had already been made based on previous correspondences between NASA and the President.

At 11:15 a.m. Pacific Time on January 5, 1972, President Nixon announced his commitment to fund the development of the Space Shuttle. Just 19 days later, his budget was presented to Congress. Necessary funding for the Space Shuttle was ultimately approved.

NASA still lacked a firm design for the Space Shuttle. Mathematica reported that two options remained economically feasible for the Booster stage. Either a large solid rocket booster system or a high-pressure liquid fueled Booster system were considered feasible.

A high-pressure liquid fueled series or parallel burn Booster was projected to cost $7 billion to develop and $100 per pound of payload to operate.

A parallel burn Booster utilizing large solid rocket boosters was projected to cost $5.5 billion to develop and $160 per pound of payload to operate.

While the Booster employing large solid rocket boosters would likely be more expensive to operate, NASA opted to take advantage of huge cost savings up front.

Since costs of ultimate operation could be absorbed throughout the life of the Space Shuttle program, the parallel burn Booster using large solid rocket boosters was selected.

On March 15, 1972, NASA officially announced plans to incorporate this design into the Space Shuttle. The solid rocket boosters were to be recovered and re-used following each launch. NASA claimed each solid rocket booster could be flown 100 to 500 times prior to retirement.

As per this parallel burn configuration, the Orbiter's engines would be ignited at launch and fed by liquid fuel contained in a large external fuel tank which would be jettisoned after the spacecraft neared orbit.

On March 17, 1972, NASA requested bids for construction of the Orbiter. Responses from Rockwell, Grumman, McDonnell Douglas and Lockheed were received by May 12, 1972.

Space Shuttle Main Engine (SSME) development remained the responsibility of Rocketdyne under a contract which had already been issued in July, 1971. NASA updated their SSME specifications and submitted them to Rocketdyne in April, 1972.

The International Space Division of Rockwell received the contract to develop and manufacture the Orbiter, as well as manage overall vehicle integration, on July 25, 1972.

By this time, the accepted design of the Space Shuttle was quite similar to the vehicles that eventually entered service. However, a few design changes would follow.

NASA made a decision to scrap two abort solid rocket motor assemblies which would have been attached to the Orbiter's tail. During an in-flight emergency, these motors would have been fired to propel the Orbiter away from its main solid rocket boosters.

It was determined that the Space Shuttle's main engines would be able to adequately guide the spacecraft away from the solid rocket boosters if a "Return-to-Launch Site" (RTLS) abort became necessary.

In addition, two turbofan engines which would have been fitted to the Orbiter's rear fuselage were scrapped. The turbofan engines would have enabled the Orbiter to maintain powered flight during landing operations and powered flight transfer between ground facilities.

Instead, NASA decided that the Orbiter could safely glide to a landing. Point-to-point flying of the Orbiter between facilities would be accomplished by carrying the spacecraft "piggyback" atop a modified Boeing 747 aircraft.

Martin Marietta was granted a construction contract for the Space Shuttle's External Tank (ET) in August, 1973. Originally, this contract specified that a small solid rocket booster be attached atop the ET.

The small solid rocket booster would be fired following ET jettison to propel the tank back toward the atmosphere. However, studies indicated that the ET could not achieve orbit on its own inertia and would fall back, then break up in the atmosphere by itself.

Thiokol Corporation was granted a contract to manufacture the Space Shuttle's Solid Rocket Boosters (SRB) in November, 1973. The company had already demonstrated a successful track record of providing reliable solid rocket boosters for a plethora of rockets.

A dispute regarding the SRB contract was initiated by Lockheed following its issuance. While the contract remained with Thiokol after a resolution of the action, the grievance process effectively froze the contract until June, 1974.

Rockwell began work on Space Shuttle Enterprise, designated Orbiter Vehicle-101 (OV-101), on June 4, 1974. All of the subcontractors delivered their Enterprise components to Rockwell by the end of 1975.

Enterprise was rolled out of the Rockwell hangar at Palmdale, California on September 17, 1976. The spacecraft was subsequently rolled to the NASA Dryden Flight Research Center at Edwards Air Force Base, California for flight testing.

Rockwell continued the development of Space Shuttles Columbia (OV-102), Discovery (OV-103) and Atlantis (OV-104). Although Enterprise was intended to be re-fitted as an operational Space Shuttle, NASA opted instead to construct Challenger (OV-099) from what was originally a high-fidelity Structural Test Article (STA-099).

NASA anticipated that its full fleet of four Space Shuttles would be in complete operation by 1984. NASA would decide to build a fifth operational Space Shuttle, Endeavour (OV-105), specifically to replace Challenger, which was lost on January 28, 1986. However, a fifth operational Space Shuttle was not originally anticipated.

NASA expected the Space Shuttle fleet to ultimately complete 25 to 60 missions per year. Plans called for up to 20 launches per year from each of three launch pads.

Although NASA reviewed several detailed proposals for constructing virgin Space Shuttle processing, launch and landing sites in various parts of the country, the space agency wisely opted to conserve scarce resources by modifying existing facilities.

The two Apollo launch pads at the Kennedy Space Center, 39A and 39B, were renovated for the Space Shuttle. A third Space Shuttle launch site was constructed at Vandenberg Air Force Base, California by renovating Titan III launch complex SLC-6, nicknamed "Slick-6", although Space Shuttles never ended up being launched from there.

One of the first important tasks of the Space Shuttle fleet was to have been to boost the Skylab space station to a higher orbit. NASA had considered renovating and occupying Skylab as a cost-effective way of starting up a "new" space station program.

When Skylab was initially abandoned on February 8, 1974 it was purposely boosted to a slightly higher orbit which varied from 269 to 283 miles. Calculations indicated that Skylab would remain in orbit for at least nine years, giving NASA ample time to get the Space Shuttle program rolling.

NASA had optimistically envisioned that a Space Shuttle would be able to attempt a docking with Skylab as early as the fifth Space Shuttle flight, which was originally expected to occur as early as the latter part of 1979.

The Skylab rescue mission was formally approved by NASA in September, 1977 and slated for the fifth Space Shuttle flight. In November, 1977 NASA awarded a contract to Martin Marietta for the design and construction of suitable docking and boost mechanisms.

By late 1978, National Oceanographic and Atmospheric Administration studies indicated that solar activity was forecast to become the second most intense in the century, with solar winds likely to be strong enough to increase atmospheric drag and cause Skylab to decay to much lower altitudes within a year.

The revelation prompted NASA to determine how, if necessary, Skylab could be guided back to Earth in a manner necessary to avoid damage to populated areas. NASA was also prompted to step up its development of Space Shuttle hardware necessary to save the space station.

Martin Marietta had already designed a teleoperator docking unit that could be remotely guided by an astronaut to dock with Skylab. Once docking was completed, engines in the docking mechanism could be fired to boost Skylab to a safe orbit.

The docking unit was scheduled to be delivered to the Kennedy Space Center by August, 1979 for a Space Shuttle flight scheduled for September, 1979. Due to development delays, the September, 1979 Space Shuttle flight would be the third, not the fifth as envisioned.

It was discovered that Skylab operational systems were working well, and NASA remained optimistic that the space station could be saved. But time was clearly running out. The effort to save Skylab ended abruptly in December, 1978.

NASA had run into development problems with the Space Shuttle Main Engines, and it became clear that even the first Space Shuttle launch would not occur until well after the solar winds had increased atmospheric drag and forced the Skylab orbit to decay beyond hope of rescue.

On December 15, 1978 NASA Administrator Robert Frosch informed President Jimmy Carter that Skylab could not be saved, and that NASA would attempt to guide the space station to a controlled re-entry as far away from populated areas as possible.

Skylab, however, would refuse to die quietly. At 3:45 a.m. EDT on July 11, 1979 controllers at the NASA Johnson Space Center commanded Skylab to tumble, hoping the space station would break apart upon re-entry. It did not, however, break apart as expected, and at 12:37 p.m. EDT on July 11, 1979 Skylab rained debris near Perth, Australia.

Although the Skylab rescue mission was never completed, the Space Shuttle fleet was slated to support the launch of a plethora of scientific, commercial and military satellites. It would also facilitate on-orbit scientific investigations and aid NASA in a slower, more methodical approach to completing a space station.

The Space Shuttle fleet was never, however, destined to perform up to 60 missions per year as intended. As NASA approached a more modest launch rate of about 24 missions per year by the late 1980's, the Space Shuttle had already proven to be much more expensive and time-consuming to service and maintain than originally envisioned.

And, the entire program was halted on January 28, 1986 when Space Shuttle Challenger exploded 73 seconds after launch. This was just the 25th Space Shuttle mission, and it became stunningly clear that major modifications to the entire Space Shuttle program were called for.

With the launch of Space Shuttle Discovery on September 29, 1988 NASA entered a brand new era of Space Shuttle operations, adopting a more relaxed pace averaging about eight launches per year. Learning from one of its greatest tragedies, NASA was able to rebuild and maintain a Space Shuttle program that has been remarkably safe and reliable, with the exception of the loss of Space Shuttle Columbia on February 1, 2003.

SPACE SHUTTLE COLUMBIA

Date of First Launch: April 12, 1981

Date of Final Launch: January 16, 2003

Number of Launches: 28

Columbia was named after the Boston-based sloop of the late 1700's, captained by Robert Gray. Other vessels named Columbia included the first U.S. Navy ship to circle the globe and the Command Module flown during Apollo 11, the first mission to land men on the Moon. Space Shuttle Columbia burned up and was destroyed on February 1, 2003 during re-entry of mission STS-107. Seven crew members perished. The cause of the failure was traced to External Tank insulation impacting the underside of Columbia during launch.

SPACE SHUTTLE CHALLENGER

Date of First Launch: April 4, 1983

Date of Final Launch: January 28, 1986

Number of Launches: 10

Challenger was named after the British naval vessel HMS Challenger that sailed the Atlantic and Pacific Oceans in the 1870's. Challenger was also the name of the Apollo 17 Lunar Module. Space Shuttle Challenger was destroyed 73 seconds after liftoff of mission STS-51L on January 28, 1986. A crew of seven perished. The cause of the accident was determined to be burn through of the right-hand Solid Rocket Booster which resulted in the explosion of the External Tank.

SPACE SHUTTLE DISCOVERY

Date of First Launch: August 30, 1984

Date of Final Launch: February 24, 2011

Number of Launches: 39

Discovery was named after one of two ships used by British explorer James Cook in the 1770's as he explored the South Pacific Ocean. Other ships also carried the name Discovery. These included a ship used by Henry Hudson as he sought a Northwest Passage between the Atlantic and Pacific Oceans in the early 1600's. Another was a ship used by the British Royal Geographic Society on an expedition to the North Pole in 1875. The organization had a follow-up ship also named Discovery in support of an Antarctic expedition in 1904.

Following its retirement in 2011, Space Shuttle Discovery was transported to the Smithsonian Institution in Washington, D.C. Discovery is currently housed in the James S. McDonnell Space Hangar at the National Air and Space Museum's Steven F. Udvar-Hazy Center in Chantilly, Virginia.

SPACE SHUTTLE ATLANTIS

Date of First Launch: October 3, 1985

Date of Final Launch: July 8, 2011

Number of Launches: 33

Atlantis was named after the primary research vessel of the Woods Hole Oceanographic Institute in Massachusetts from 1930 to 1966. Following its retirement in 2011, Atlantis was moved to the Kennedy Space Center Visitors Complex. Space Shuttle Atlantis is currently on display in a multi-million dollar facility at the complex.

SPACE SHUTTLE ENDEAVOUR

Date of First Launch: May 7, 1992

Date of Final Launch: May 16, 2011

Number of Launches: 25

Endeavour was named after one of two ships captained by James Cook. Endeavour's maiden voyage was in 1768 in an exploration of the South Pacific Ocean. For the first time, a Space Shuttle Orbiter's name was selected via a national competition of elementary and secondary schools. The name Endeavour was announced by President George H.W. Bush in 1989.

Following its retirement in 2011, Space Shuttle Endeavour was transported to Los Angeles. After a three-day tow through the streets of Los Angeles, Endeavour found its new home inside the Samuel Oschin Space Shuttle Display Pavillion at the California Science Center. Endeavour is currently on permanent public display at the facility.

The following information is more or less common to all Space Shuttles. Although the Space Shuttle program was retired in 2011, this information is included here for historic and research purposes.

The Space Shuttle Orbiter is constructed in major sections. These include:

1. The Forward Fuselage, which is made up of lower and upper sections that form a clamlike shell around

a pressurized crew compartment. It houses the crew compartment and supports the forward reaction control system module, nose cap, nose gear wheel well, nose gear, nose gear doors and forward Orbiter/External Tank attachment.

2. The Crew Compartment, which is a pressurized three-level compartment intended to support all astronaut activities aboard the Orbiter. The Crew Compartment has a side hatch for normal crew ingress and egress which can be blown in an emergency.

The Crew Compartment also contains a hatch into an airlock from the middeck, and a hatch from the airlock through the aft bulkhead into the payload bay to support either spacewalks or access to pressurized modules in the payload bay area.

The Crew Compartment has 11 windows, including six forward windows, two overhead rendezvous observation windows, two aft payload bay viewing windows and a single side hatch window. Three panes make up each window. At a total width of nearly three inches, these are the thickest windows ever designed for see-through flight applications.

The Crew Compartment contains three levels, including a flight deck located at the top, a middeck in the center and a lower level equipment bay. The Crew Compartment is pressurized at 14.7 pounds per square-inch with an atmosphere of 80% nitrogen and 20% oxygen. This accommodates the crew with a shirt-sleeve working environment.

3. The Airlock, which is typically housed in the crew compartment middeck. The Airlock is 83 inches long and has a diameter of 63 inches. Two pressurized sealing hatches and a complement of support system hardware are contained in the Airlock. Each sealing hatch has a four-inch diameter observation window.

Depending on the mission application, the Airlock can be positioned in either the crew compartment or the payload bay in support of spacewalk activities. The Airlock can also be modified to employ a tunnel adapter hatch, tunnel adapter and tunnel to allow the crew to enter pressurized modules in the payload bay.

4. The Wings, which provide an aerodynamic lifting surface to produce conventional lift and control for the Orbiter. The left and right Wings consist of the wing glove and an intermediate section that includes the main landing gear wells.

The Wings also include a torque box, a forward spar for mounting the reusable leading edge structure thermal protection system, the wing/elevon interface, the elevon seal panels and the elevons, which provide flight control during atmospheric flight. Each Wing is 60 feet long and has a maximum thickness of 5 feet.

5. The Midfuselage, which provides a structural interface for the forward fuselage, aft fuselage and wings. It supports the payload bay doors, hinges, tie-down fittings, forward wing glove as well as various Orbiter system components. The Midfuselage provides the structural foundation for the payload bay.

6. The Payload Bay Doors, which are opened shortly after orbit is achieved to allow heat to be released from the Orbiter and to allow the release of payloads as necessary. The two Payload Bay Doors are hinged at the port or starboard side of the midfuselage and are latched at the centerline atop the Orbiter.

Thermal seals on the Payload Bay Doors provide a relatively airtight environment within the payload bay when the doors are closed. This seal is critical when ground operations require equipment and payloads to be maintained within the payload bay. Each Payload Bay Door is 60 feet long by 15 feet wide.

7. The Aft Fuselage, which consists of an outer shell, thrust structure and internal secondary structure. The Aft Fuselage supports and interfaces with the left-hand and right-hand aft orbital maneuvering system/reaction control system pods.

The Aft Fuselage also supports and interfaces with the wing aft spars, midfuselage, Orbiter/External Tank rear attachments, Space Shuttle Main Engines, aft heat shield, body flap, vertical tail and two pre-launch umbilical panels.

The Aft Fuselage outer shell allows access to systems installed within the structure. The Aft Fuselage thrust structure supports the three Space Shuttle Main Engines and their hardware. The Aft Fuselage internal secondary structure houses hardware and wiring for auxiliary power unit, hydraulics, ammonia boiler and flash evaporator systems.

8. The Orbital Maneuvering System/Reaction Control System Pods, which are attached to the upper aft fuselage left and right sides and contain all of the Orbital Maneuvering System (OMS) and Reaction Control System (RCS) propulsion elements that are located at the aft of the Orbiter.

9. The Body Flap, which provides a thermal shield for the three Space Shuttle Main Engines during re-entry and provides the Orbiter with pitch control trim during atmospheric flight.

10. The Vertical Tail, which consists of a structural fin surface, a rudder/speed brake surface, a tip and a lower trailing edge. The Vertical Tail provides aerodynamic stability for the Orbiter during flight, and its rudder can be split into two halves to act as a speed brake during landing.

The Space Shuttle Orbiter remains the most complex flying machine ever built, and is made up of operational systems which include:

1. The Thermal Protection System, which consists of various materials that are applied to the Orbiter external skin to help maintain the skin at acceptable temperatures during flight. Additional thermal protection is provided by insulation installed inside the Orbiter.

Thermal protection materials protect the Orbiter from all temperatures above 350 degrees Fahrenheit experienced during ascent and re-entry. These materials also protect the Orbiter in a range of temperatures from minus 250 degrees Fahrenheit to 3,000 degrees Fahrenheit experienced while in orbit.

A number of different materials are used in the Thermal Protection System, including reinforced carbon-carbon, black high-temperature reusable surface insulation tiles, black fibrous refractory composite insulation tiles, white low-temperature reusable surface insulation tiles, quilted insulation blankets and more specialized materials.

2. The Main Propulsion System, which is made up of the three Space Shuttle Main Engines and all of their related hardware. These include the Orbiter Main Propulsion System Helium Subsystem, Main Propulsion System Propellant Management Subsystem, External Tank interfaces and Pogo Suppression System.

In addition, the Main Propulsion System includes Space Shuttle Main Engine controllers, malfunction detection systems, hydraulic systems, thrust vector control systems and helium, oxidizer and fuel flow sequence systems.

3. The Orbiter/External Tank Separation System, which contains all of the hardware and control systems necessary to support safe separation of the External Tank from the Orbiter. This is made up of two 17-inch disconnects, an External Tank separation system and two Orbiter umbilical doors.

4. The Orbital Maneuvering System, which is made up of two Orbital Maneuvering System engines and all of their related hardware. One Orbital Maneuvering System engine is housed in each of two Orbital Maneuvering System (OMS)/Reaction Control System (RCS) pods attached to the top aft end of the Orbiter.

Each OMS engine burns a combination of monomethyl hydrazine and nitrogen tetroxide liquid fuel, and can produce a thrust of 6,000 pounds. Each OMS engine can be gimbaled to provide pitch and yaw control for the

Orbiter as it maneuvers toward its intended mission orbit.

5. The Reaction Control System, which is made up of thrusters fired to help the Orbiter achieve a precise orbital path or perform changes in its position, and all of their related hardware. Thrusters are located at the forward end of the Orbiter and in each of the two aft Orbital Maneuvering System (OMS)/Reaction Control System (RCS) pods.

The RCS contains a total of 38 primary thrusters and 6 vernier thrusters. The forward RCS array contains 14 primary thrusters and two vernier thrusters. A total of 12 primary thrusters and two vernier thrusters are housed in each of the two OMS/RCS pods.

Each RCS thruster burns a combination of monomethyl hydrazine and nitrogen tetroxide liquid fuel. Each primary thruster can produce a thrust of 870 pounds, while each vernier thruster can produce a thrust of 24 pounds. The RCS thrusters can be fired in a plethora of combinations depending on the specific mission requirements.

6. The Electrical Power System, which provides the Orbiter with electricity. The Electrical Power System is made up of the Power Reactant Storage and Distribution Subsystem, the Fuel Cell Power Plants and the Electrical Power Distribution and Control Subsystem.

The Power Reactant Storage and Distribution Subsystem stores and delivers liquid oxygen and liquid hydrogen fuel to three Fuel Cell Power Plants. In burning the liquid oxygen and liquid hydrogen, the Fuel Cell Power Plants are each capable of producing 21,000 watts of continuous output, plus 15-minute peaks of up to 36,000 watts.

Electrical power produced by the Fuel Cell Power Plants is distributed and regulated by the Electrical Power Distribution and Control Subsystem. Prior to launch, Orbiter electricity is provided by ground systems and the Fuel Cell Power Plants. The Fuel Cell Power Plants assume full control of Orbiter power at launch minus 3.5 minutes.

7. The Environmental Control and Life Support System, which controls and regulates the astronaut life support functions of the Orbiter. Life support functions include crew compartment pressure, cabin air revitalization, water cooling, temperature control, water supply, waste collection, airlock support and crew altitude protection.

8. The Auxiliary Power Unit System, which is a storable liquid hydrazine-fueled, turbine-driven power unit that generates mechanical shaft power to drive a hydraulic pump that produces hydraulic pressure for the Orbiter hydraulic system.

The Auxiliary Power Unit System is vital to the Orbiter, since it controls hydraulic devices that gimbal the Space Shuttle Main Engines, operate various propellant valves in the Space Shuttle Main Engines and move the Orbiter elevons, body flap and rudder speed brake.

In addition, the Auxiliary Power Unit System controls devices that retract the External Tank/Orbiter 17-inch disconnects, deploy and retract the landing gear and support the braking and steering of the Orbiter at landing.

The Auxiliary Power Unit System is made up of three Auxiliary Power Units (APU) located in the aft fuselage. Each APU is identical, but each is operated independently of the others. All three APU's are started five minutes before launch, and are turned off shortly before the Orbiter reaches orbit.

One APU is started shortly before the Orbiter makes its de-orbit burn, with the remaining two APU's started just after the de-orbit burn is completed. All three APU's run until the Orbiter completes its landing and roll-out.

9. The Water Spray Boiler System, which cools the Auxiliary Power Unit (APU) lubrication oil and hydraulic fluid. Three independent Water Spray Boilers each serve a corresponding APU. The Water Spray Boiler System sprays water onto the APU lubrication oil and hydraulic fluid lines, thus cooling the fluids within them.

10. The Hydraulic System, which distributes the hydraulic pressure produced by the Auxiliary Power Unit (APU) System. The Hydraulic System is made up of three independent hydraulic systems, each of which is mated to a corresponding APU.

11. The Landing Gear System, which is a conventional aircraft tricycle configuration landing gear consisting of a single forward nose landing gear and a left and right main landing gear. Each landing gear includes a shock strut with two tire and wheel assemblies.

Each main landing gear wheel is equipped with a brake assembly with anti-skid protection. The nose landing gear is steerable. The landing gear are retracted and deployed by hydraulic mechanism, and are locked in position within a wheel well and protected by landing gear doors when not in use.

12. The Caution and Warning System, which is designed to warn the crew of any conditions that may adversely affect the performance of the Orbiter. The Caution and Warning System primarily consists of a set of visual and aural alarms that alert the crew when any system has exceeded or strayed from its operational limits.

13. The Orbiter Lighting System, which provides both interior and exterior lighting for the Orbiter. Interior lighting is used primarily to support crew operations. Exterior lighting is used primarily to illuminate the payload bay area in order to aid visibility during payload operations and spacewalks.

14. The Smoke Detection and Fire Suppression System, which is designed to warn the crew of any fires, as well as protect the Orbiter from any fires that might develop. The system is made up of smoke detectors, portable fire extinguishers and automatic fire extinguishers.

15. The Payload Deployment and Retrieval System, which includes an electromechanical arm that maneuvers a payload from the payload bay and back again, plus all of its related hardware. This is more commonly known as the Remote Manipulator System (RMS), and is operated by the crew from inside the Orbiter.

The RMS can remove payloads from the payload bay for deployment. It can also grapple free-flying payloads and berth them back in the payload bay. It has been used to grapple satellites and the Hubble Space Telescope for repair and redeployment.

The RMS has also acted as an aid to astronauts participating in spacewalks. It has been used as a mobile extension ladder, work station and foot restraint for astronauts working in the payload bay during spacewalks. Cameras attached to the RMS have also been used to aid astronauts in visual inspections of the payload bay area.

16. The Payload Retention System, which is made up of a wide variety of hardware used to keep payloads secure within the payload bay. The Payload Retention System is designed to provide three-axis support for up to five separate payloads per mission.

17. The Communications System, which consists of all the equipment necessary to support the flow of voice and data transmissions to and from the Orbiter. Primary communications to and from the Orbiter flow through the NASA Space Flight Tracking and Data Network and the Tracking and Data Relay Satellite System.

The Communications System incorporates a huge and complex network of communications equipment and instrumentation. In addition to allowing both visual and aural communication with the crew, the Communications System supports a constant flow of data regarding the performance of the Orbiter, its systems and its position.

18. The Avionics System, which controls or assists in the control of most Orbiter systems. Primary functions

of the Avionics System include automatic determination of Space Shuttle operational readiness, plus sequencing and control of the Solid Rocket Boosters and External Tank during launch and ascent.

The Avionics System also monitors the performance of the Orbiter, supports digital data processing, communications and tracking, payload and system management, guidance, navigation and control, as well as the electrical power distribution for the Orbiter, External Tank and Solid Rocket Boosters.

The Avionics System is made up of more than 300 computer black boxes located at various positions in the Orbiter, connected by about 300 miles of electrical wiring. A number of redundant hardware and software back-ups are incorporated within the Avionics System due to its critical nature.

Remarkably, the Avionics System is so complex that it can support fully automatic flight of the Space Shuttle from launch through landing. Although the Space Shuttle is typically guided to the runway manually during landing, the Avionics System can perform all flight functions automatically, with the exception of on-orbit rendezvous.

19. The Purge, Vent and Drain System, which is designed to produce gas purges that help regulate Orbiter temperature, prevent the accumulation of hazardous gases, vent unpressurized compartments during ascent and re-entry, drain any excess trapped fluids and keep window cavities clear.

The Purge, Vent and Drain System is made up of three separate sets of distribution plumbing located throughout the Orbiter. Purge gas consists of cool, dry air and gaseous nitrogen. Using a number of purge ports and vents, the system maintains constant humidity and temperature and assures that contaminants cannot enter the Orbiter.

20. The Orbiter Flight Crew Escape System, which is a system designed to allow the crew to escape the Orbiter under a variety of flight situations. The system consists of an Inflight Crew Escape System, Emergency Egress Slide and Secondary Emergency Egress hardware.

The Inflight Crew Escape System, introduced after the Challenger accident, allows the crew to bail out of the Orbiter during flight. It will not, however, allow the crew to escape under circumstances similar to the Challenger accident. To use this system, the Orbiter must be on a level glide path.

The specific scenario under which astronauts might benefit from the Inflight Crew Escape System would be if the Orbiter could for some reason not reach a runway. Since astronauts might not survive either a water or land ditching of the Orbiter, the Inflight Crew Escape System does provide significant advantages.

Using the Inflight Crew Escape System, the astronauts would first blow the side hatch door. They would then deploy an escape pole, which extends from the inside to the outside of the Orbiter. The astronauts would then each use hardware attached to their space suits to slide along the escape pole, then parachute to safety.

Should the astronauts need to escape the Orbiter after performing a landing, an Emergency Egress Slide can be deployed out the side hatch after the hatch is blown or opened manually. Secondary Emergency Egress is provided by blowing the left overhead window, after which hardware allows astronauts to be safely lowered to the ground.

The Space Shuttle Orbiter has proven itself to be a versatile, reliable vehicle capable of carrying out a number of tasks.

Employing a payload bay measuring 60 feet long by 15 feet wide, the Orbiter was designed to carry payloads into space and perform missions at orbital altitudes ranging from 115 to 250 miles.

Payload capability averaged about 37,800 pounds per mission, but under certain conditions heavier payloads could be carried. An Orbiter performing a mission at a lower altitude would be able to carry a heavier payload than one performing a mission at a higher altitude.

Given Space Shuttle performance enhancements like lighter weight External Tanks and improved Main Propulsion System, Space Shuttle payload capability peaked at about 60,000 pounds.

The Orbiter was designed to carry a maximum crew of eight astronauts, although it could carry up to ten astronauts in an emergency. The Orbiter carried all of the supplies and equipment necessary for the crew to perform its mission.

The mission duration of the Orbiter was typically seven to nine days, although certain Orbiters were modified to allow missions of up to 16 days. The Orbiter afforded its occupants a shirt-sleeve environment, and never produced stresses in excess of three g's, which is less than many amusement park thrill rides.

The Orbiter was launched in an upright position, with thrust provided by three Space Shuttle Main Engines (SSME) and two Solid Rocket Boosters (SRB). SRB separation occurred about two minutes after launch, and the SSME's burned for about 8.5 minutes after launch.

The SSME's shut down just before the Orbiter reached orbit. The External Tank (ET) that provided fuel for the SSME separated from the Orbiter shortly after SSME cutoff. Combinations of the 38 reaction control thrusters and six vernier thrusters are fired to stabilize the Orbiter during ET separation and helped clear the Orbiter from the ET.

Combinations of the reaction control thrusters and vernier thrusters are also fired to support attitude pitch, roll and yaw maneuvers as the Orbiter continued its ascent after ET separation. The two orbital maneuvering system engines were then fired to place the Orbiter on its proper orbit.

Once the Orbiter reached its proper orbit, the orbital maneuvering system engines could be fired again to support any major velocity maneuvers that became necessary. Combinations of the reaction control thrusters and vernier thrusters could be fired to support precision operations such as rendezvous and docking operations.

Once the mission was completed, the orbital maneuvering system engines were fired to slow the Orbiter in what is called the deorbit burn, or deorbit maneuver. Once in orbit, the Orbiter travelled at a speed of about 25,400 feet per second. The deorbit burn decreased the Orbiter speed to about 300 feet per second as it prepared for re-entry.

The unpowered Orbiter then re-entered the atmosphere, and is guided to a precision landing like a traditional aircraft. There were three Space Shuttle landing sites available in the United States. These were located at the Kennedy Space Center in Florida, Edwards Air Force Base in California and White Sands in New Mexico.

Once on the ground, a number of highly specialized vehicles approached the Orbiter to perform a variety of servicing and safety tasks prior to crew egress. Great care was taken to provide for the safety of the crew and prevent toxic fuels and gases from harming the environment.

The Orbiter was then routinely serviced for its next mission in a turnaround that typically took two to three months. In certain circumstances, the Orbiter was ferry-flown to California for factory modifications or major servicing.

In the event an emergency was encountered during flight, the Orbiter had several flight options available. These included:

1. Return To Launch Site (RTLS), in which the Orbiter could return to the Kennedy Space Center if all thrust was lost from one Space Shuttle Main Engine (SSME) between liftoff and launch plus 4 minutes, 20 seconds, after which time there was not enough fuel available to support this type of abort.

An RTLS abort consisted of a powered stage, at which time the SSME's were still firing. This would be followed by an External Tank separation stage, which could not occur until after the Solid Rocket Boosters were jettisoned. Finally, the Orbiter could be maneuvered into a glide stage for a return to the launch site.

2. Transatlantic Abort Landing (TAL), in which the Orbiter could land at an overseas abort landing site if a Space Shuttle Main Engine (SSME) failed after the last RTLS abort opportunity but before any other abort could be accomplished. The TAL abort would also be attempted if an Orbiter system failure prevented any other type of abort.

Using the TAL abort, the Orbiter could complete a powered flight on a ballistic path across the Atlantic Ocean, and would then perform a glide landing at a pre-selected runway located in either the city of Moron in Spain, the city of Dakar in Senegal or the city of Ben Guerur in Morocco.

3. Abort To Orbit (ATO), in which the Orbiter could reach a lower, but safe, orbit if a propulsion failure did not allow it to reach its intended orbit. An ATO was performed during Space Shuttle Mission STS-51F, in which Challenger was able to successfully complete its mission at a lower orbital altitude.

4. Abort Once Around (AOA), in which the Orbiter could travel once around the Earth before making a landing in the United States. The AOA would be used if a propulsion failure did not allow the Orbiter to maintain any orbit, even one lower than intended.

The AOA would also be used if for some reason a system failure required the Orbiter to land quickly after it reached orbit. For all intents and purposes, an AOA would be performed in a similar manner to a normal re-entry and landing.

5. Contingency Abort, which would be used if the Orbiter could not land on a runway. During a Contingency Abort, the Orbiter would ideally be guided to a safe glide path to allow the astronauts to use the Inflight Crew Escape System. If a safe glide path was not possible, the Orbiter would have to be ditched with the crew aboard.

The Space Shuttle Orbiter has proven itself to be a versatile vehicle, and has supported a number of diverse mission applications. These have included the deployment of a variety of scientific, military and commercial satellites and the deployment of scientific space probes.

A vast number of scientific investigations have been conducted aboard Space Shuttle Orbiters, including those performed inside pressurized laboratory modules housed in the Orbiter payload bay. Many scientific payloads have been carried in the Orbiter payload bay, including free-flying satellites that were deployed and retrieved.

Many scientific accomplishments have been made through spacewalks conducted from the Orbiter. In addition to rehearsing construction techniques for the International Space Station, astronauts have demonstrated that on-orbit repair and maintenance of satellites is possible, as are a number of on-orbit troubleshooting activities.

Space Shuttle Orbiters also have completed an ambitious docking program with the Russian Mir Space Station and the International Space Station, helping to extend an unprecedented continuous U.S. presence in space while ushering in a new era of international cooperation in space.

SPACE SHUTTLE EXTERNAL TANK

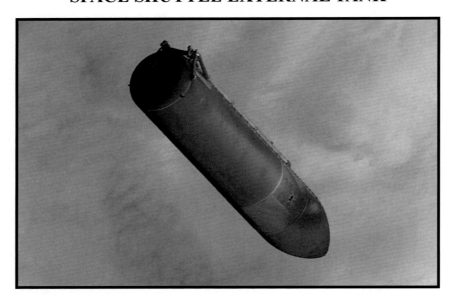

Length: 153 feet, 10 inches

Diameter: 27 feet, 7 inches

The External Tank (ET) was the only non-reusable element of the Space Shuttle. It was also the largest element of the Space Shuttle, and provided the structural backbone of the entire system. The chief purpose of the ET was to carry the liquid fuels necessary to provide power for the Orbiter's three main engines.

Martin Marietta (later Lockheed Martin) won a competitive contract to design and manufacture the Space Shuttle ET in 1973. The contract specified that the ET be constructed at the NASA Michoud Assembly Facility in New Orleans, Louisiana.

The Michoud plant afforded ample space to support construction of ET's, plus deep-water port access to allow transportation of ET's by enclosed barge to the Kennedy Space Center. Completed ET's were individually barged to the Kennedy Space Center in a voyage that typically took 4 to 5 days.

For many years, the ET barge was towed to and from the Kennedy Space Center by leased tug. In 1998, however, NASA opted to save money by introducing a policy of towing the ET barge to and from the Kennedy Space Center by one of the Solid Rocket Booster (SRB) retrieval ships, whose crews would otherwise have remained idle.

The first ET was delivered to NASA on September 7, 1977. This was not a flight-ready ET, but rather was used for tests in association with the Space Shuttle Main Propulsion Test Article (MPTA-098) assembled at the Rockwell plant at Palmdale, California. Three test ET's were ultimately delivered to NASA.

The first flight-ready ET was delivered to NASA on June 29, 1979. The first six ET's delivered to NASA were called the Standard Weight Tank (SWT), with each tank weighing 75,500 pounds. SWT's were flown on Space Shuttle Missions STS-1 through STS-5 and STS-7.

During Space Shuttle Missions STS-1 and STS-2, the ET's were painted white. NASA quickly determined that hundreds of pounds of weight and thousands of dollars in preparation work would be saved if the ET's remained unpainted, and so all ET's flown from STS-3 onward remained unpainted, sporting an orange-brown color.

In 1979, even before a Space Shuttle had completed a space flight, NASA issued a directive that ET's be lightened by at least 6,000 pounds so that Space Shuttles would be able to carry proportionally heavier payloads.

The resulting ET was called the Lightweight Tank (LWT) which was made 10,000 pounds lighter than the SWT through several methods, including materials and design changes and the use of new fabrication techniques. The 65,500-pound LWT was first flown on Space Shuttle Mission STS-6, and then from STS-8 through STS-90.

Beginning with Space Shuttle Mission STS-91, a new ET called the Super Lightweight Tank (SLWT) were flown. At a weight of 58,000 pounds, the SLWT is 7,500 pounds lighter than the LWT. The SLWT was introduced primarily to allow NASA to carry heavier payloads aboard the Space Shuttle in support of International Space Station construction.

Weight savings in the SLWT were created primarily by constructing the ET from an aluminum-lithium alloy. Previous versions of the ET were constructed using an aluminum-steel alloy and titanium. In general terms, however, much about all three versions of the ET were identical.

Each ET was comprised of a liquid oxygen tank located at the top and a liquid hydrogen tank located at the bottom. The liquid oxygen tank was connected to the liquid hydrogen tank by an intertank, which was located in between the other two.

The intertank was designed to receive and distribute all thrust loads that the SRB's produce during launch and flight. The intertank was able to absorb and transfer these loads evenly, providing vital structural integrity for the Space Shuttle. The intertank was 22 feet, 6 inches long by 27 feet, 7 inches wide.

The liquid oxygen tank was 54 feet, 7 inches long by 27 feet, 7 inches wide and carried 145,138 gallons of liquid oxygen weighing 1,380,000 pounds. The liquid hydrogen tank was 96 feet, 8 inches long by 27 feet, 7 inches wide and carried 390,139 gallons of liquid hydrogen weighing 230,000 pounds.

Fully loaded with a total of 1,610,000 pounds of liquid fuel, the SLWT version of the ET weighed 1,668,000 pounds at liftoff. Liquid oxygen was stored aboard the ET at a temperature of -297 degrees Fahrenheit, while the liquid hydrogen was stored aboard the ET at a temperature of -423 degrees Fahrenheit.

Since the liquid fuels stored inside the ET were this cold, the outer surface of the ET required thermal protection. This was provided by a one inch layer of spray-on foam insulation applied over the forward portion of the liquid oxygen tank, the intertank and the sides and bottom of the liquid hydrogen tank.

This foam insulation was intended to reduce ice or frost formation on the tank, which could both increase the weight of the ET and become hazardous to the Space Shuttle during launch. The foam insulation also served to protect the ET from the effects of engine and aerodynamic heating, which could potentially cause the liquid fuel to boil.

An ablative coating made of material that flakes off as it becomes hot was applied to the ET external bulges and projections to protect them from aerodynamic heating that developed during flight.

The ET also contained systems that were necessary to support its operation. These included a pressurization and vent system to regulate the tank pressure, an environmental conditioning system to regulate the temperature and humidity of the intertank area and an electrical system to distribute power and provide lightning protection.

Much of this equipment is housed in the intertank. All fluid control mechanisms and valves that regulate performance of the ET, with the exception of the vent control valves, were located in the Orbiter. This was due to the cost savings over replacing this equipment after every Space Shuttle mission, since the ET could not be recovered.

The ET supplied liquid oxygen and liquid hydrogen to the Orbiter's three main engines through 17-inch diameter feed lines. The liquid oxygen was fed at a rate of 159,480 pounds, or 16,800 gallons, per minute while the liquid hydrogen was fed at a rate of 26,640 pounds, or 45,283 gallons, per minute.

At launch, the ET was attached to both the Orbiter and SRB's. The SRB's were jettisoned from the ET about two minutes after launch. The ET typically emptied about 8.5 minutes after launch, at which time it was detached from the Orbiter, broke up and fell into a predetermined area of either the Pacific or Indian Ocean.

SPACE SHUTTLE SOLID ROCKET BOOSTERS

Length: 149 feet, 2 inches

Diameter: 12 feet, 2 inches

The vast majority of thrust needed to launch the Space Shuttle was provided by two Solid Rocket Boosters (SRB). SRB's were manufactured by the Wasatch Division of Morton Thiokol Corporation, located in Brigham City, Utah.

In addition to providing the bulk of Space Shuttle liftoff thrust, the SRB's supported the entire weight of the Orbiter and External Tank (ET) prior to launch. The Space Shuttle SRB's were the largest solid-fueled motors ever built, and the first designed to be reused.

Each SRB weighed about 1,300,000 pounds at launch. The solid fuel contained in the SRB weighed about 1,100,000 pounds while the inert weight of each SRB was about 200,000 pounds.

The primary elements of each SRB were the motor, structure, separation system, operational flight instrumentation, recovery system, pyrotechnics, deceleration system and range safety destruct system.

Each SRB was attached to the ET at the SRB's aft frame by two lateral sway braces and a diagonal attachment. The forward end of each SRB was attached to the ET at the forward end of the SRB's forward skirt.

On the launch pad, Each SRB was fastened to the Mobile Launcher Platform (MLP) at the SRB aft skirt by four large bolts and nuts that were severed by small explosive charges at liftoff.

The propellant mixture in each SRB was made up of 69.6% ammonium perchlorate oxidizer, 16% aluminum fuel, 0.4% iron oxide catalyst, 12.04% polymer binder and 1.96% epoxy curing agent.

The propellant was contained within the SRB beginning with an 11-point star-shaped perforation in the forward segment to a double-truncated cone perforation in both of the aft segments and the aft closure segment.

These varying shapes allowed the SRB thrust to be reduced by about 33% at launch plus 50 seconds. This reduction in thrust was intended to alleviate stress to the Space Shuttle as it entered its area of maximum dynamic pressure during ascent.

The SRB's employed during each Space Shuttle mission were matched pairs, each made up of four solid rocket motor segments. To minimize any thrust imbalance, the SRB pairs were matched by loading each of the four SRB segments in pairs using the same batches of solid fuel.

The segmented solid rocket motor design assured maximum flexibility during manufacturing operations, and also ease of transportation. The SRB's were transported to the launch site using heavy-duty rail cars equipped with special SRB covers.

The cone-shaped aft skirt of each SRB provided one of the most vital supports for the Space Shuttle prior to launch, since it could react to loads that might shift between the SRB's and the MLP during pre-launch operations.

Four SRB separation motors were also mounted on the aft skirt of each SRB. The aft section of each SRB contained avionics and a thrust vector control system that consisted of two auxiliary power units, hydraulic pumps, hydraulics systems and a nozzle extension jettison system.

The forward section of each SRB contained avionics, a sequencer, four forward separation motors, a nose cone separation system, drogue and main parachutes, recovery beacon, recovery light, range safety system and, in certain flights, a parachute camera system.

Each SRB had two integrated electronic assemblies, one at the forward and one at the aft. These assemblies provided the electronic command connections to initiate and control various functions of SRB components during flight.

The SRB's were ignited by electronic command from the Orbiter at Launch Minus Zero, provided that the Space Shuttle Main Engines (SSME) had built up enough thrust to support a launch.

The SSME's were ignited first, since the SRB's could not be shut down once they were ignited. The results would be catastrophic if the SRB's were ignited after an SSME failure on the launch pad.

Also at Launch Minus Zero, the four bolts which held each SRB to the MLP were blown by explosive charges. Each bolt measured 28 inches long by 3.5 inches in diameter.

Each SRB could produce a thrust of about 3,300,000 pounds of thrust at liftoff. The combined thrust of the SRB's accounted for just over 70% of the total thrust needed to carry the Space Shuttle into space. Each SRB exhaust nozzle could be gimbaled up to eight degrees to help steer the Space Shuttle during ascent.

About 125 seconds after launch and at an altitude of about 150,000 feet, the SRB's burned out and were jettisoned from the ET. The jettison command originated from the Orbiter, and jettison occurred when the forward and aft attach points between the SRB's and ET were blown by explosive charges.

Milliseconds after SRB separation, 16 solid-fueled separation motors, four in the forward section of each SRB and four in the aft skirt of each SRB, were fired for just over one second to help carry the SRB's away from the rest of the Space Shuttle. Each of the separation motors could produce a thrust of about 22,000 pounds.

The SRB's continued to ascend in a slow, tumbling motion for about 75 seconds after SRB separation, to a maximum altitude of about 220,000 feet. The SRB's then began to quickly fall toward the Atlantic Ocean.

About 225 seconds after SRB separation and at an altitude of about 15,700 feet the nose cap of each SRB was ejected, which resulted in deployment of a pilot parachute. The pilot parachute had a diameter of 11.5 feet, and provided the force necessary to activate mechanisms which pulled the drogue parachute from its stored position.

The drogue parachute had a diameter of 54 feet, and was used to orient and stabilize the descent of each SRB to a tail-first attitude in preparation for the deployment of the main parachutes. About 248 seconds after SRB separation and at an altitude of about 6,000 feet, deployment of the main parachutes began.

Three main parachutes were deployed on each SRB. Each main parachute had a diameter of 136 feet. The main parachutes accompanied each SRB to water impact, which occurred about 295 seconds after SRB separation at a speed of about 81 feet per second.

The SRB's impacted the Atlantic Ocean about 140 miles from the launch site. Since each SRB impacted the water nozzle-first, air trapped within the SRB casings caused each SRB to float with its forward end extended about 30 feet out of the water.

Crews aboard specialized SRB retrieval ships quickly set about locating each SRB by homing in on radio beacon signals transmitted from each SRB. Crews could also be aided in locating the SRB's by flashing lights activated on each SRB.

Once located, the crews began recovering each SRB, plus the drogue parachutes and main parachutes. The SRB nozzles were then plugged, the solid rocket motors dewatered and the SRB's towed back horizontally to a receiving and processing site on Cape Canaveral Air Force Station.

There, each SRB was removed from the water. After a set of thorough inspections, the SRB components were disassembled and washed with fresh and deionized water to limit saltwater corrosion. Refurbishing of each SRB then began, with some components sent back to the manufacturer and some components remaining at the launch site.

SPACE SHUTTLE MAIN ENGINES

Length: 14 feet

Diameter: 7 feet, 6 inches

Space Shuttle Main Engines (SSME) were the most advanced liquid-fueled rocket engines ever built. They were manufactured by the Rocketdyne Division of Rockwell, located at Canoga Park, California.

Each Space Shuttle Orbiter had three SSME's mounted on the aft fuselage in a triangular pattern. Each SSME was designed for 7.5 hours of operation over an average lifespan of 55 starts.

SSME's burned a combination of liquid oxygen and liquid hydrogen fed from the Space Shuttle External Tank (ET). The SSME's employed a staged combustion cycle, in which the fuels were first partially burned at high pressure and low temperature, then burned completely at high pressure and high temperature.

The staged burning of fuel allowed the SSME's to produce thrust more efficiently than other rocket engines. A rapid burning of fuel in a staged burn gave SSME's a combustion efficiency of about 99%.

SSME thrust was variable, which was extremely important in Space Shuttle mission applications. SSME thrust could be varied from a range of 65% minimum to 109% maximum of their 100% rated power levels at precise increments of 1% as needed.

A thrust value of 100%, called rated power, corresponded to a thrust of 375,000 pounds per each SSME at sea level, or 470,000 pounds of thrust per each SSME in a vacuum.

A thrust value of 104%, called full power, which was typically employed as the Space Shuttle ascended, corresponded to a thrust of 393,800 pounds per each SSME at sea level, or 488,800 pounds of thrust per each SSME in a vacuum.

In an emergency, each SSME could be throttled up to 109% power. This corresponded to a thrust of 417,300 pounds of thrust per each SSME at sea level, or 513,250 pounds of thrust per each SSME in a vacuum.

All three SSME's received identical throttle commands at the same time. Throttle commands usually came from general purpose computers aboard the Orbiter. In an emergency, however, throttle commands could be controlled manually from the flight deck.

Firing of the three SSME's began at Launch Minus 6.6 seconds, at which time general purpose computers aboard the Orbiter commanded a staggered start of each SSME. The first to fire was Main Engine Number Three (right), followed by Main Engine Number Two (left) and Main Engine Number One (center) at intervals of 120 milliseconds.

If all three SSME's did not reach a mandatory thrust of 90% over the course of the next three seconds, a Main Engine Cutoff command was initiated automatically, followed by the cutoff of all three SSME's and a number of safety functions.

If all three SSME's were performing normally, the Space Shuttle could be launched. The SSME's achieved full power at launch, but were throttled back at about Launch Plus 26 seconds in order to protect the Space Shuttle from aerodynamic stress and excessive heating.

The SSME's were throttled back up to full power at about Launch Plus 60 seconds, and typically continued to produce full power until shortly before the Space Shuttle reached orbit. During ascent, each SSME could be gimbaled plus or minus 10.5 degrees pitch and yaw to help steer the Space Shuttle.

The SSME's typically burned for about 8.5 minutes after launch. At about Launch Plus 7 minutes, 40 seconds the SSME's were throttled down so that the Space Shuttle would not experience gravitational force in excess of three g's. Gravitational forces in excess of three g's might adversely affect the Space Shuttle and its crew.

At about ten seconds before Main Engine Cutoff (MECO), a MECO sequence began. About three seconds later, the SSME's were commanded to begin throttling back at intervals of 10% thrust per second until they reached a thrust of 65% of rated power, called minimum power. Minimum power was maintained for just under seven seconds, then the SSME's shut down.

The SSME's were controlled during flight by digital computer systems mounted on each engine. These operated in conjunction with engine sensors, valve actuators and spark igniters to provide a redundant, self-contained system for monitoring engine control, checkout and status.

The SSME digital computer systems, called Main Engine Controllers, were mounted on the top of each SSME, on the outside of the combustion chamber. Each SSME had one Main Engine Controller, which consisted of two digital computers and their related electronics.

In association with general purpose computers aboard the Orbiter, the SSME Main Engine Controllers were able to provide flight readiness verification, engine start and shutdown sequencing, closed-loop thrust and propellant mixture ratio control and sensor operation.

The Main Engine Controllers also produced valve actuator and spark igniter control signals, performed engine performance monitoring and limiting functions, responded to Orbiter commands plus transmitted and stored engine status, performance and maintenance data.

Following MECO, the SSME's had completed their function and were no longer needed during a Space Shuttle mission. SSME's were thoroughly inspected, checked and tested after each Space Shuttle flight. Each SSME could be replaced or changed out as necessary.

On rare occasions, SSME's were static tested on the launch pad in what is called a Flight Readiness Firing (FRF). An FRF was typically performed when engines that had never been flown were to be used for the first time during a Space Shuttle mission. In a typical FRF, all three SSME's were simultaneously fired for about ten seconds.

PENGUIN

Classification: Ship-to-Ship Cruise Missile

Length: 9 feet, 10 inches

Diameter: 11 inches

Wingspan: 4 feet, 7 inches

Mk 1 Range: 13 miles

Mk 2 Range: 19 miles

Date of First Cape Canaveral Launch: February 18, 1982

Date of Final Cape Canaveral Launch: April 8, 1982

Number of Cape Canaveral Launches: 9

A ship-to-ship missile designed by the Norwegian Defense Research Establishment, the Penguin missile was manufactured in the early 1960's with the assistance of U.S. research and test facilities, including the range at Cape Canaveral.

The Penguin employed a fully passive guidance system, since radio signals from the parent ship or the missile itself could be easily jammed during at-sea operations.

A warhead system originally designed for the U.S. Bullpup missile was adapted for use on the Penguin. The warhead was built for the Penguin in Europe under U.S. license.

The Penguin was deployed from a box-type launcher attached to a ship-board deck mount. Prior to launch, each missile remained attached to the ship by an umbilical connection. A total of six Penguin missiles were carried aboard Norwegian Storm Class fast patrol boats.

174

Targets were detected by ship-board instrumentation. Appropriate data was loaded directly to the Penguin's guidance system, which functioned independently of the ship once the missile was launched.

The Penguin's box-type launcher was opened as the parent ship turned away. Once launched, the missile's pre-programmed inertial guidance system, coupled with an infrared heat detector, provided automatic homing toward its target.

The missile also had the capability of homing in on a target using a passive direction finder which sensed an enemy's electromagnetic signature.

An improved version of the Penguin, called the Penguin Mk 2, added an active radar homing head to improve guidance toward a target. The Penguin Mk 2 was deployed on missile boats operated by Norway, Sweden, Greece, Turkey and the U.S.

In the early 1970's, the Penguin Mk 2 was modified to create a short-range ballistic missile. This version of the Penguin was used for fixed coastal defense as well as land-based mobile-launcher applications.

In the mid-1970's, the missile was further adapted under a joint agreement between Norway and Sweden. These nations converted the Penguin Mk 2 to an F-16 fighter-based air-to-surface missile.

However, only the ship-to-ship version of the Penguin was ever launched using range facilities at Cape Canaveral.

PERSHING II

Classification: Intermediate-Range Ballistic Missile

Length: 34 feet, 10 inches

Diameter: 3 feet, 4 inches

Finspan: 6 feet, 9 inches

Range: 1,100 miles

Date of First Cape Canaveral Launch: July 22, 1982

Date of Final Cape Canaveral Launch: March 21, 1988

Number of Cape Canaveral Launches: 49

By the 1970's, the U.S. Army and contractor Martin Marietta were prepared to develop an improved version of the Pershing IA called the Pershing II.

Based upon the original Pershing missiles, the Pershing II contained technological and operational improvements which resulted in greater range and accuracy.

Accuracy was dramatically improved with the addition of a Goodyear radar area correlation guidance system. The device compared oncoming targets with images recorded in computer memory.

Since the Pershing II was more accurate than the Pershing I and Pershing IA, it was considered capable of causing at least as much damage to a specific target while carrying a smaller weapons payload.

For this reason, the nuclear warhead capability of the Pershing II was reduced to 50 kilotons compared to 400 kilotons for the Pershing I and Pershing IA.

In addition, the Pershing II was equipped with an advanced, deadly ground-penetrating warhead which could cause considerable damage even to reinforced or underground structures.

Production of the Pershing II was stepped up in the mid to late 1970's in response to an increasing Soviet deployment of intermediate to long-range mobile land-based missiles.

The first Pershing II test launch occurred on July 22, 1982 from Cape Canaveral Launch Complex 16. A total of 108 Pershing II missiles were subsequently deployed in West Germany from May, 1983 through December, 1985.

Test launches for troop training at Cape Canaveral continued as well. A total of six Pershing II missiles were launched from Launch Complex 16 in just one day, setting the record for land-based same-day launches from the Cape.

Although the Pershing II represented the first operational IRBM for the U.S. Army since being stripped of the Jupiter missile by the "Wilson Memorandum" in 1956, this capability was to be short-lived.

In 1987, U.S. President Ronald Reagan and Soviet Premier Mikhail Gorbacev signed the Intermediate Nuclear Forces (INF) Treaty. The treaty banned all land-based intermediate-range missiles, including the Pershing II.

Pershing II missiles would be dismantled and destroyed. Those rendered inert and kept on display, including one at the Air Force Space and Missile Museum at Cape Canaveral, would remain open to random Soviet inspection.

The U.S. Army had again lost its IRBM capability, but by treaty rather than memorandum.

TITAN 34D

Classification: Space Launch Vehicle

Length: 160 feet, 9 inches

Diameter: 10 feet

Date of First Cape Canaveral Launch: October 30, 1982

Date of Final Cape Canaveral Launch: September 4, 1989

Number of Cape Canaveral Launches: 8

Still quite similar to the Titan III-C on which it was based, the Titan 34D was introduced in 1982 and could incorporate either the Transtage third stage or a new upper stage called an Inertial Upper Stage (IUS).

The IUS was a two-stage booster which effectively provided a third and fourth stage that allowed the Titan 34D to carry large military payloads into orbit.

Performance of the Titan 34D was also improved by adding a one-half segment to the previous generation of Titan III solid rocket boosters, making a total of five and one-half segments per booster.

The two resulting United Technologies solid rocket boosters burned Powered Aluminum/Ammonium Perchlorate solid fuel and could produce a combined thrust of 2,498,000 pounds.

The first stage Aerojet engine could produce a thrust of 532,000 pounds. An Aerojet second stage engine could produce a 101,000-pound thrust. Both the first and second stage engines burned Aerozine 50/Nitrogen Tetroxide liquid fuel.

The IUS first stage could produce a thrust of 62,000 pounds, while its second stage was capable of producing a 26,000-pound thrust. Both IUS stages were solid-fueled.

The Titan 34D was able to carry a 27,500-pound payload to low-Earth orbit or a 4,200-pound payload to geostationary transfer orbit.

TRIDENT II

Classification: Fleet Ballistic Missile

Note: Fleet Ballistic Missiles are also referred to as Submarine-Launched Ballistic Missiles.

Length: 44 feet

Diameter: 6 feet, 11 inches

Range: 5,000 miles

Date of First Cape Canaveral Launch: January 15, 1987

Date of Final Cape Canaveral Launch: Active

Number of Cape Canaveral Launches: Active

The Trident II D5 missile program was initiated in October, 1980 under what was known as the Phase I demonstration and validation of the U.S. Navy Submarine Launched Ballistic Missile (SLBM) modernization program.

This was a plan for selecting an advanced SLBM which would be deployed not later than 1989 with the ultimate goal of phasing out all other less advanced submarine-based missiles.

The resulting Trident II D5, which was designed to use existing Trident I launch tubes, is a potent three-stage missile which provides the backbone of U.S. nuclear offensive capability.

As was the case with the Poseidon C3 and Trident I C4, which are referred to as Poseidon and Trident I, the Trident II D5 may be accurately referred to simply as Trident II because only one version of the missile was ever deployed.

All three stages of the Trident II are solid-fueled, with more sophisticated guidance and a more potent weapons payload than any previous SLBM.

While the first two stages are constructed with graphite epoxy, the Trident II introduced a third stage made of Kevlar which provided substantial weight savings.

The Trident II employs an Avco stellar-aided inertial guidance system. Much about the missile, including its exact range and destructive capability, remains classified because of its status as an active weapons system.

LOFT 1

Classification: Research Rocket

Length: 10 feet, 3 inches

Diameter: 8 inches

Finspan: 2 feet, 5 inches

Date of First Cape Canaveral Launch: November 17, 1988

Date of Final Cape Canaveral Launch: November 17, 1988

Number of Cape Canaveral Launches: 1

Described as a "little rocket with a big mission", LOFT-1 was built by E-Prime Aerospace Corporation of Titusville, Florida. Although it was technically a sounding rocket, which are not typically included in official Cape Canaveral launch chronologies, the launch of LOFT-1 was one of the most significant, if smallest, launches in the history of the Cape.

Entrepreneurs at E-Prime Aerospace Corporation had envisioned a number of rockets with payload capabilities ranging from 675 pounds to 20,300 pounds which could be introduced as early as late 1990. The company's decision to develop these rockets was precipitated by a far-reaching post-Challenger tragedy decision by NASA to stop launching commercial payloads.

The decision by NASA opened up a virgin U.S. commercial launch industry, and E-Prime Aerospace Corporation sought an early jump on its competitors at exploiting the Cape Canaveral infrastructure for commercial purposes. In order to determine how difficult planning and executing a commercial launch at the Cape would be, the company built its LOFT-1 rocket, standing for Launch Operations Flight Test-1.

Launch of LOFT-1 was targeted for October, 1987 but a mountain of paperwork caused the launch to be postponed until November 17, 1988. Even so, LOFT-1 earned the distinction of being the first fully commercial launch in the history of Cape Canaveral, managing to beat the firmly-rooted Atlas, Delta and Titan rocket families at this task.

The LOFT-1 motor and airframe were built by Vulcan Systems of Colorado Springs, Colorado. The rocket was divided into three sections - a solid-fueled rocket motor at the bottom, a parachute section in the middle and a payload section at the top. The solid-fueled rocket motor was capable of producing a liftoff thrust of 15,602 pounds.

Following launch, the solid-fueled rocket motor burned for just 4.4 seconds, capable of boosting the rocket to a speed of about 1,400 feet-per-second. The rocket maintained an unpowered coast for another 25 seconds until reaching its highest altitude of about 14,500 feet. The rocket then began falling toward the Atlantic Ocean, with the solid-fueled rocket motor separating from the rocket at an altitude of about 14,000 feet. A one-foot diameter drogue parachute opened at an altitude of about 10,000 feet, followed by a larger main parachute at an altitude of about 4,000 feet.

Splashdown was intended to occur about two miles downrange of the launch site, where recovery operations would begin. LOFT-1 carried four scientific experiments representing three universities and two high schools. Although the parachute system failed to operate properly and the payload section was damaged upon water impact, the experiments were successfully recovered.

Although E-Prime Aerospace Corporation had surprised many by its ability to beat established rocket manufacturers in conducting the first commercial rocket launch from Cape Canaveral, the company itself never got off the ground. Unfortunately, LOFT-1 represented the company's first and final launch.

DELTA II 6000 SERIES

Classification: Space Launch Vehicle

Length: 128 feet

Diameter: 8 feet

Date of First Cape Canaveral Launch: February 14, 1989

Date of Final Cape Canaveral Launch: July 24, 1992

Number of Cape Canaveral Launches: 16

Based largely on the Delta 4000 Series rockets already in use, the Delta II 6000 Series improved performance over previous Delta rockets by incorporating nine improved Castor solid rocket boosters.

Six of the solid rocket boosters were ignited at liftoff, with the remaining three ignited following burnout and jettison of the first six. The basic nine-booster Delta II flight profile has not changed since.

The two-stage Delta II 6000 Series rocket, designated Delta II 6920, could carry an 8,780-pound payload to low-Earth orbit.

The three-stage version, designated Delta II 6925, could carry a 3,190-pound payload to geostationary transfer orbit.

TITAN IVA

Classification: Space Launch Vehicle

Length: 177 feet, 2 inches (with IUS upper stage)

Length: 187 feet, 2 inches (maximum with no upper stage)

Length: 207 feet, 2 inches (with Centaur upper stage)

Diameter: 10 feet (first and second stages)

Diameter: 16 feet, 8 inches (payload fairing)

Date of First Cape Canaveral Launch: June 14, 1989

Date of Final Cape Canaveral Launch: August 12, 1998

Number of Cape Canaveral Launches: 14

Billed as "assured access to space" by the U.S. Air Force, the Titan IVA was introduced for the specific purpose of carrying large military satellites into space. By the mid-1980's it became clear that the Space Shuttle fleet could not handle as many military payloads as originally planned. The Titan IVA was intended to supplement the Space Shuttle fleet as conditions warranted. As many as two launches per year were envisioned from Cape Canaveral Launch Complex 41, which was renovated to support the vehicle.

Originally referred to simply as Titan IV, the first version of the rocket was renamed Titan IVA to distinguish it from an improved version introduced in 1997 as the Titan IVB. Titan IV development began in 1984 under the U.S. Air Force Complementary Expendable Launch Vehicle (CELV) program. At the time, the CELV program called for a total of 10 launch vehicles which would all employ Centaur third stage boosters.

Initial launch capability for the rocket, at first simply called CELV, was targeted for October, 1988 following U.S. Air Force development approval granted in October, 1984. Full development funding for contractor Martin Marietta was secured by June, 1985. The production contract was modified in 1985 to incorporate a second launch configuration using the existing Inertial Upper Stage (IUS) third stage booster.

Originally intended as a back-up launch vehicle for the Space Shuttle to be used only as conditions warranted, the first completed CELV rockets were to be placed in storage until needed. However, the explosion of Space Shuttle Challenger on January 28, 1986 dramatically changed the face of the CELV program. After the tragic loss of Challenger and subsequent stand-down of the Space Shuttle fleet, the U.S. Air Force faced an emergency need for a reliable launch vehicle to carry their large military satellites.

In August, 1986, the U.S. Air Force approved a major restructuring of the CELV program, which was officially renamed Titan IV. A total of 23 launch vehicles were ordered. The Titan IV design was also modified to include a two-stage version. This restructure also incorporated the capability of launching polar-orbit Titan IV missions from Vandenberg Air Force Base, California Space Launch Complex-4 East. An overall rate of six Titan IV launches per year was established.

During this post-Challenger restructuring process, NASA decided to abandon development of a powerful wide-body Centaur upper stage which was deemed too hazardous to carry aboard Space Shuttles. Since this version of the Centaur upper stage, once completed, could be launched aboard Titan IV rockets, development of this upper stage was taken over by Martin Marietta under U.S. Air Force supervision.

By 1988, additional modifications to the Titan IV program emerged. A decision was made to develop improved solid rocket motors to increase payload capability. These would be phased in after Titan IV launches using existing booster technology had occurred.

The U.S. Air Force also decided to purchase an additional 18 rockets, rounding out a planned Titan IV fleet of 41 launch vehicles. This expansion precipitated the renovation of Launch Complex 40 at the Cape, providing a total of three launch sites for the Titan IV.

With its first launch on June 14, 1989, the Titan IV fleet began to solidify as a program with five vehicle configurations, three launch sites and a potential mission rate of up to eight launches per year.

Although several military payloads were carried aboard Space Shuttles following their return to flight, a policy decision by the U.S. Air Force dictated that the Space Shuttle would be abandoned as a means of delivering military satellites. This solidified the role of the Titan IV as a vital fixture in military space operations.

Like the Commercial Titan III, the Titan IV was based on the Titan 34D. Titan IVA flew with two United Technologies solid rocket motors (SRM). Each seven-segment SRM was 112 feet, 11 inches tall and 10 feet wide. These SRM could produce a combined thrust of 3,200,000 pounds.

However, the United Technologies SRM for the Titan IVA were slated to eventually be replaced by new and improved SRM manufactured by Hercules Aerospace Products. The so-called Solid Rocket Motor Upgrade (SRMU) could improve Titan IVA performance by about 25 percent. The SRMU upgrade eventually resulted in the introduction of a new Titan IV variant named Titan IVB.

An Aerojet dual chamber first stage engine could produce a thrust of 542,600 pounds. An Aerojet second stage engine was capable of producing a 106,000-pound thrust. Both the first and second stage engines burned Aerozine 50/Nitrogen Tetroxide liquid fuel.

Five distinct versions of the Titan IV were created to handle a broad variety of military payloads and mission objectives. These variants are numbered Versions 401 through 405.

VERSION 401

Specifically incorporating the Centaur third stage, Titan IV Version 401 was designed to carry satellites to geostationary orbit.

The Centaur third stage burned liquid oxygen/liquid hydrogen fuel and could produce a thrust of 33,000 pounds.

Titan IV Version 401 could be launched with a 66-foot, 76-foot or 86-foot tall fairing depending upon specific payload applications.

With the United Technologies SRM, Titan IV Version 401 could carry a maximum 10,000-pound payload to geostationary orbit.

This version was launched exclusively from Cape Canaveral.

VERSION 402

Specifically incorporating the Inertial Upper Stage (IUS) upper stage, Titan IV Version 402 was designed to carry satellites to low-Earth orbit. A standard 56-foot tall payload fairing is employed.

The solid-fueled IUS was made up of two separate stages, effectively providing four-stage capability for the Titan IV. The IUS first stage could produce a thrust of 41,600 pounds, while the IUS second stage could produce a thrust of 17,630 pounds.

With the United Technologies SRM, Titan IV Version 402 could carry a maximum 38,780-pound payload to low-Earth orbit.

This version was launched exclusively from Cape Canaveral.

VERSION 403

One of three two-stage versions of the Titan IV carrying no upper stage (NUS), Titan IV Version 403 was designed specifically to support polar-orbit missions launched exclusively from Vandenberg Air Force Base, California.

Titan IV Version 403 could fly with either a 56-foot or 66-foot tall payload fairing. With the United Technologies SRM, Titan IV Version 403 could carry a 31,100-pound payload to low-Earth orbit.

VERSION 404

The second NUS version of the Titan IV, Version 404 also was designed to support polar-orbit missions launched exclusively from Vandenberg Air Force Base, California.

Using a standard 50-foot tall payload fairing, Titan IV Version 404 could carry a 29,600-pound payload to low-Earth orbit with the United Technologies SRM.

VERSION 405

The third and final NUS version of the Titan IV, Version 405 was designed to support low-Earth orbit missions launched exclusively from Cape Canaveral.

Carrying either a 56-foot or 66-foot tall payload fairing, Titan IV Version 405 could carry a 39,100-pound payload to low-Earth orbit with the United Technologies SRM.

An improved version of the Titan IV called the Titan IVB was introduced in February, 1997. Following the debut of the Titan IVB, the original version of the Titan IV was renamed Titan IVA.

Since a number of Titan IVA rockets remained in the Air Force inventory after the debut of the Titan IVB, both rockets were launched until the last Titan IVA was launched from Cape Canaveral on August 12, 1998.

DELTA 4000 SERIES

Classification: Space Launch Vehicle

Length: 128 feet

Diameter: 8 feet

Date of First Cape Canaveral Launch: August 27, 1989

Date of Final Cape Canaveral Launch: June 12, 1990

Number of Cape Canaveral Launches: 2

The Delta 4000 Series was to have been the last generation of the Delta family at a time when virtually all commercial, civilian and military satellite delivery duties were being transferred to the multi-purpose Space Shuttle.

However, in the early 1980's McDonnell Douglas proposed improvements to the Delta 3000 Series with the goal of being able to carry a 3,000-pound payload to geostationary transfer orbit.

Although the Delta program was waning at the time, this goal was indeed met by increasing the first stage burn time and incorporating other technical innovations.

The same nine Castor solid rocket boosters used in the Delta 3000 Series were used in the Delta 4000 Series, but in the Delta 4000 Series configuration six of the solid rocket boosters were typically ignited at launch, with the remaining three solid rocket boosters ignited following burnout and jettison of the first six.

The Delta 3000 Series first stage RP-1 (kerosene) liquid fuel tank was extended by 4 feet, 3 inches and the liquid oxygen fuel tank was extended by 7 feet, 3 inches for incorporation in the Delta 4000 Series. Extending the fuel tanks allowed the Delta 4000 Series rockets to carry more fuel, thus extending the burn time of the first stage and improving performance.

In the first departure from the "straight-eight" Delta configuration introduced over a decade earlier, the Delta 4000 Series introduced a payload fairing adapted from the Titan III-C program. This payload fairing had a maximum diameter of ten feet, allowing added room for larger payloads.

The Delta 4000 Series also introduced improvements to the rocket to make it stronger and more durable, such as increasing the skin thickness of a number of component parts.

The increased length of the Delta 4000 Series rockets over previous Delta variants required expensive modifications to support structures at Cape Canaveral and Vandenberg Air Force Base. While these expenses may have seemed risky, the McDonnell Douglas investment on the Delta 4000 Series would prove to be very fruitful.

Although Delta production officially ceased in 1984 following 24 years of service as a workhorse of the civilian, commercial and military satellite launch industry, the Delta retirement would be short-lived.

COMMERCIAL TITAN III

Classification: Space Launch Vehicle

Length: 144 feet, 7 inches (with single payload)

155 feet, 2 inches (with dual payload)

Diameter: 10 feet

Date of First Cape Canaveral Launch: December 31, 1989

Date of Final Cape Canaveral Launch: September 25, 1992

Number of Cape Canaveral Launches: 4

Introduced in 1989 to meet the needs of commercial clients, the Commercial Titan III featured several major improvements over the Titan 34D upon which it was based.

The Commercial Titan III could carry one payload or two separate payloads at the same time. It also employed upgraded first and second stage engines and enhanced solid rocket boosters.

Two United Technologies solid rocket boosters were able to produce a combined thrust of 2,800,000 pounds. Each solid rocket booster was 90 feet, 5 inches tall and 10 feet, 2 inches wide.

The Aerojet dual chamber first stage engine could produce a thrust of 547,950 pounds, while an Aerojet second stage engine could produce a 105,000-pound thrust. Both the first and second stage engines burned Aerozine 50/Nitrogen Tetroxide liquid fuel.

The Commercial Titan III could incorporate several different third stages depending upon the individual requirements for each customer and payload application.

Third stages available to be flown on the Commercial Titan III included the Inertial Upper Stage (IUS), Centaur G-Prime, Transfer Orbit Stage (TOS), Payload Assist Module (PAM) and Expendable Shuttle Compatible Orbit Transfer System (ESCOTS).

Additional flexibility for customers included the ability of the Commercial Titan III to carry up to two payloads at the same time. In the dual payload mode, the payload fairing separated into halves at about four and one-half minutes into the flight.

The first payload was deployed about one hour into the flight, while the second payload was deployed about two and one-half hours into the flight.

In general terms, although the specific performance capabilities of the available upper stages varied, the Commercial Titan III was able to carry a single 31,530-pound payload or combined 32,430-pound dual payload to low-Earth orbit.

In other applications, the Commercial Titan III could carry a 25,740-pound payload to space station transfer orbit or a 10,980-pound payload to geostationary transfer orbit.

Able to support the launches of NASA planetary spacecraft, the Commercial Titan III could carry a 7,480-pound payload on a lunar trajectory or a 5,720-pound payload on a Mars or Venus trajectory.

DELTA II 7000 SERIES

Classification: Space Launch Vehicle

Length: 128 feet

Diameter: 8 feet

Date of First Cape Canaveral Launch: November 26, 1990

Date of Final Cape Canaveral Launch: September 10, 2011

Number of Cape Canaveral Launches: 94

The Delta II 7000 Series improved performance by employing new solid rocket boosters.

Lightweight Hercules (later Alliant Techsystems) Graphite Epoxy solid rocket boosters, larger and more powerful than previously employed Castor solid rocket boosters, improved the overall vehicle thrust. The solid rocket boosters were called Graphite Epoxy Motors (GEM).

Each GEM was 42 feet, 6 inches long and had a diameter of 3 feet, 4 inches. Each GEM burned HTPB solid fuel. The GEM's ignited on the ground, or "ground-lit" GEM's, could each produce a thrust of about 112,200 pounds. The GEM's ignited in the air, or "air-lit" GEM's, could each produce a thrust of about 116,100 pounds.

A Rocketdyne first stage engine could produce a liftoff thrust of about 200,000 pounds. Like previous Delta variants, the first stage burned a combination of liquid oxygen and RP-1 (kerosene) liquid fuel.

An Aerojet second stage engine burned a combination of nitrogen tetroxide and Aerozine-50 liquid fuel. The second stage engine could produce a thrust of about 9,815 pounds. Several Delta II 7000 Series rockets were available with two stages only, and were used for carrying payloads into low-Earth orbit.

Payload capability of the two-stage variants depended on the number of GEM's employed and the size of the payload fairing, which was offered in diameters of 9 feet, 6 inches or 10 feet. The heaviest payloads could be carried using the smaller, lighter payload fairing.

The Delta II 7320 employed three GEM's and with the 9-foot, 6-inch diameter payload fairing could carry a maximum 6,320-pound payload to low-Earth orbit.

The Delta II 7420 employed four GEM's and with the 9-foot, 6-inch diameter payload fairing could carry a maximum 6,970-pound payload to low-Earth orbit.

The most powerful of the two-stage Delta II 7000 Series rockets, designated Delta II 7920, employed nine GEM's and could carry an 11,330-pound payload to low-Earth orbit using the 9-foot, 6-inch payload fairing.

A number of three-stage versions of the Delta II 7000 series were available to meet diverse mission applications. All of the three-stage variants employed a Thiokol solid-fueled third stage that could produce a thrust of about 14,920 pounds.

As with the two-stage variants, performance of the three-stage Delta II 7000 Series rockets depended upon the number of GEM's employed and the size of the payload fairing, which was offered in diameters of 9 feet, 6 inches or 10 feet. The heaviest payloads could be carried employing the smaller, lighter payload fairing.

The Delta II 7325 employed three GEM's, and with the 9-foot, 6-inch diameter payload fairing could carry a maximum 2,210-pound payload to geostationary transfer orbit or a maximum 1,615-pound payload to Earth-escape trajectory.

The Delta II 7425 employed four GEM's, and with the 9-foot, 6-inch diameter payload fairing could carry a maximum 2,490-pound payload to geostationary transfer orbit or a maximum 1,770-pound payload to Earth-escape trajectory.

The Delta II 7925 employed nine GEM's, and with the 9-foot, 6-inch diameter payload fairing could carry a maximum 4,120-pound payload to geostationary transfer orbit or a maximum 2,900-pound payload to Earth-escape trajectory.

STARBIRD

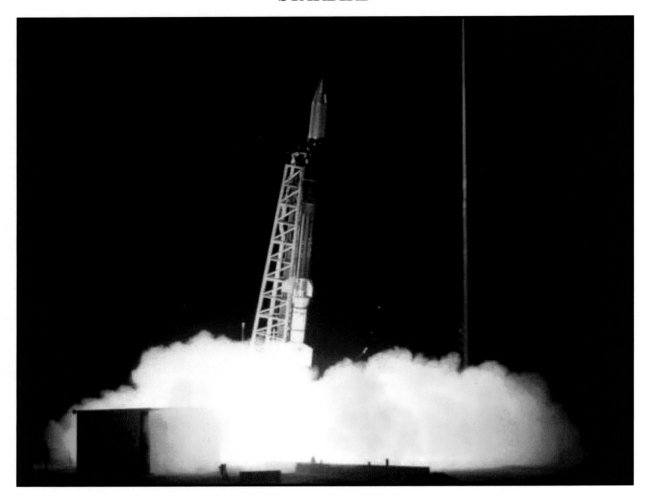

Classification: Research Rocket

Length: 57 feet

Date of First Cape Canaveral Launch: December 18, 1990

Date of Final Cape Canaveral Launch: May 28, 1993

Number of Cape Canaveral Launches: 3

Starbird was a four-stage, solid fueled rocket built by Orbital Sciences Corporation in support of the U.S. Strategic Defense Initiative program. The suborbital rocket was designed to look like a ballistic missile in flight, so that strategic space, air and land-based assets could be tested to see if they could identify potential threats. The rocket had a range of about 300 miles.

ATLAS I-CENTAUR

Classification: Space Launch Vehicle

Length: 137 feet, 10 inches (with medium fairing)

Length: 144 feet (with large fairing)

Diameter: 10 feet

Date of First Cape Canaveral Launch: April 18, 1991

Date of Final Cape Canaveral Launch: April 25, 1997

Number of Cape Canaveral Launches: 10

Introduced in 1987, the Atlas I-Centaur employed two Rocketdyne booster engines capable of producing a combined thrust of 377,500 pounds. A Rocketdyne sustainer engine provided 60,500 pounds of thrust.

Two Rocketdyne vernier engines provided an additional thrust of 669 pounds each. The booster, sustainer and vernier engines all burned liquid oxygen/RP-1 (kerosene) liquid fuel.

With the medium fairing, the Atlas I-Centaur could carry a 13,000-pound payload to low-Earth orbit, a 5,150-pound payload to geosynchronous transfer orbit or a 3,350-pound payload to Earth-escape trajectory.

With the large fairing, the Atlas I-Centaur could carry a 12,550-pound payload to low-Earth orbit, a 4,950-pound payload to geosynchronous transfer orbit or a 3,100-pound payload to Earth-escape trajectory.

PROSPECTOR

Classification: Research Rocket

Length: 46 feet

Date of First Cape Canaveral Launch: June 18, 1991

Date of Final Cape Canaveral Launch: June 18, 1991

Number of Cape Canaveral Launches: 1

Prospector was a short-lived rocket program of Orbital Sciences Corporation. It was launched just once from Cape Canaveral, carrying the NASA Joust-1 science payload. The mission was intended to be high-altitude and suborbital. The mission was unsuccessful, with the rocket being destroyed by the Range Safety Officer after veering off course very early into its flight.

ARIES I

Classification: Research Rocket

Length: 29 Feet

Date of First Cape Canaveral Launch: August 20, 1991

Date of Final Cape Canaveral Launch: October 14, 1991

Number of Cape Canaveral Launches: 2

Aries I was a solid-fueled rocket built by Orbital Sciences Corporation. The rocket was launched twice in support of Strategic Defense Initiative Office (SDIO) research efforts. The launches were conducted under the Red Tigress program, an effort to identify and track enemy missiles. Red Tigress I was launched on August 20, 1991. The mission was a failure as the rocket developed severe guidance difficulties and was destroyed by the Range Safety Officer and Launch Plus 23 seconds.

Launch of Red Tigress II was delayed as a result, but was successfully conducted on October 14, 1991. Tracking Field Experiments (TFE) were successfully completed during Red Tigress II. In addition to tracking multiple small payloads and decoys, the TFE experiments established a stabilized track of the rocket's plume using lasers and cameras.

Little is known about the Aries I rocket itself, with the exception of sketchy details about its components. The rocket consisted of a Talos first stage, Sergeant second stage and M57A1 third stage. The first stage was unguided and employed wind weighing techniques through second stage ignition. The second stage was guided by a combination of air and jet vanes mounted on the aft skirt.

The third stage was guided by a nozzle control unit and four steerable nozzles. The rocket employed separation systems utilizing pyrotechnics release for the three stages, and also the nose separation and deployment of the payload. Both the rocket and the payload utilized standardized guidance and attitude control.

ATLAS II-CENTAUR

Classification: Space Launch Vehicle

Length: 149 feet, 7 inches (with medium fairing)

Length: 155 feet, 10 inches (with large fairing)

Diameter: 10 feet

Date of First Cape Canaveral Launch: December 7, 1991

Date of Final Cape Canaveral Launch: July 25, 1996

Number of Cape Canaveral Launches: 9

The Atlas II-Centaur was developed in 1989 specifically to support the launches of U.S. Air Force Defense Support Communications Satellite (DSCS) payloads.

The vehicle employed two Rocketdyne booster engines which provided a combined thrust of 408,000 pounds. One Rocketdyne sustainer engine provided an additional 60,500 pounds of thrust at liftoff. All of the lower stage engines burned liquid oxygen/RP-1 (kerosene) liquid fuel. In a departure from all previous Atlas applications, the Atlas II-Centaur did not carry vernier engines.

Rather, the interstage which connected the Centaur second stage with the rocket's lower stages housed two hydrazine-fueled modules. Each module contained two thruster units which could produce 100 pounds of thrust each. These interstage thrusters performed the roll and velocity trim stabilization functions previously handled by vernier engines.

An Integrated Apogee Boost Subsystem was employed specifically as an additional upper stage for DSCS satellite operations. This stage operated with twin Marquardt engines producing 110 pounds of thrust each.

The overall Integrated Apogee Boost Subsystem was 27 feet long and 9 feet, 6 inches wide and burned MMH and MON3 propellant. This booster was spin-stabilized at 30 revolutions per minute and was controlled by the satellite payload itself.

With the medium fairing, the Atlas II-Centaur could carry a 14,950-pound payload to low-Earth orbit, a 6,100-pound payload to geosynchronous transfer orbit or a 4,270-pound payload to Earth-escape trajectory.

With the large fairing, the Atlas II-Centaur could carry a 14,500-pound payload to low-Earth orbit, a 5,900-pound payload to geosynchronous transfer orbit or a 4,020-pound payload to Earth-escape trajectory.

ATLAS IIA-CENTAUR

Classification: Space Launch Vehicle

Length: 149 feet, 7 inches (with medium fairing)

Length: 155 feet, 10 inches (with large fairing)

Diameter: 10 feet

Date of First Cape Canaveral Launch: June 10, 1992

Date of Final Cape Canaveral Launch: December 4, 2002

Number of Cape Canaveral Launches: 24

Identical to the Atlas II-Centaur in all other respects, the Atlas IIA-Centaur featured an upgraded Centaur second stage designed to increase payload capacity.

With the medium fairing, the Atlas IIA-Centaur could carry a 15,700-pound payload to low-Earth orbit, a 6,400-pound payload to geosynchronous transfer orbit or a 4,620-pound payload to Earth-escape trajectory.

With the large fairing, the Atlas IIA-Centaur could carry a 15,250-pound payload to low-Earth orbit, a 6,200-pound payload to geosynchronous transfer orbit or a 4,370-pound payload to Earth-escape trajectory.

PEGASUS XL

Classification: Space Launch Vehicle

Date of First Cape Canaveral Launch: February 9, 1993

Date of Final Cape Canaveral Launch: Active

Number of Cape Canaveral Launches: Active

Making effective application of Air-Launched Ballistic Missile (ALBM) research conducted decades earlier by a number of aerospace contractors, Orbital Sciences Corporation succeeded in creating an air-launched space launch vehicle called Pegasus XL.

Like an ALBM, the Pegasus XL rocket is dropped from an aircraft and fired seconds later. But instead of completing a ballistic trajectory to carry a weapons payload to its target like an ALBM, the Pegasus XL carries a payload into space.

An Alliant Techsystems Orion 50SXL solid rocket motor serves as the Pegasus XL first stage. The first stage is 33 feet, 8 inches long and has a diameter of 4 feet, 2 inches. The first stage burns HTPB solid fuel and can produce a thrust of 163,247 pounds.

An Alliant Techsystems Orion 50XL solid rocket motor serves as the Pegasus XL second stage. The second stage is 10 feet, 2 inches long and has a diameter of 4 feet, 2 inches. The second stage burns HTPB solid fuel and can produce a thrust of 34,515 pounds.

An Alliant Techsystems Orion 38 solid rocket motor serves as the Pegasus XL third stage. The third stage is 4 feet, 5 inches long and has a diameter of 3 feet, 2 inches. The third stage burns HTPB solid fuel and can produce a thrust of 7,155 pounds.

An optional fourth stage called Hydrazine Auxiliary Propulsion System (HAPS) is available for the Pegasus XL, and can provide precision orbital insertion capability for the payload. The HAPS fourth stage burns hydrazine liquid fuel.

Another optional fourth stage for the Pegasus XL is the Thiokol Star 27 solid rocket motor, which burns HTPB solid fuel and can provide Earth-escape trajectory capability for the payload.

The Pegasus XL employs a standard payload fairing which is 7 feet long and has a diameter of 3 feet, 8 inches. The Pegasus XL payload fairing is able to accommodate one payload in a dedicated launch configuration or two payloads in a shared launch configuration.

In a typical mission profile without a fourth stage, the Pegasus XL is dropped over open water from a customized L-1011 aircraft (early Pegasus XL rockets were dropped from B-52 aircraft) flying at an altitude of 38,000 feet. The drop is considered to be the actual launch, although the first stage is not fired until five seconds later.

The first stage is fired five seconds after launch when the Pegasus XL is at an altitude of 37,640 feet. The rocket employs an inertial guidance system to pitch it upward after the first stage is ignited. The first stage burns out 77 seconds after launch, and is jettisoned.

The second stage is fired 95 seconds after launch. This is followed by separation of the payload fairing at 111 seconds after launch. The second stage burns out 168 seconds after launch, at which time the second and third stage combination begin an unpowered coast period.

During this coast period, the second stage remains attached to provide aerodynamic stability. Ultimately, the spent second stage is jettisoned and the third stage is fired 592 seconds after launch. The third stage burns out 657 seconds after launch and is jettisoned from the payload, having successfully inserted it into orbit.

Although a variety of stage combinations and orbital insertions are available to meet specific mission requirements, the Pegasus XL is able to carry a maximum 1,000-pound payload to low-Earth orbit or a maximum 275-pound payload on an Earth-escape trajectory.

ATLAS IIAS-CENTAUR

Classification: Space Launch Vehicle

Length: 149 feet, 7 inches (with medium fairing)

Length: 155 feet, 10 inches (with large fairing)

Diameter: 10 feet

Date of First Cape Canaveral Launch: December 15, 1993

Date of Final Cape Canaveral Launch: August 31, 2004

Number of Cape Canaveral Launches: 27

In all other respects identical to the Atlas IIA-Centaur, the innovative Atlas IIAS-Centaur introduced a significant modification to the Atlas family.

For the first time, solid rocket boosters were mounted on the Atlas first stage to provide a dramatic increase in payload capacity. A total of four Thiokol Castor IVA solid rocket boosters were strapped to the base of rocket.

Each solid rocket booster was 37 feet long and 3 feet, 4 inches wide and could produce a thrust of about 100,000 pounds at liftoff. The boosters burned HTPB solid fuel.

Two of the solid rocket boosters were ignited at liftoff. These "ground-lit" boosters burned out about one minute into the flight and were jettisoned by spring action about 30 seconds later.

The two remaining "air-lit" solid rocket boosters were ignited about ten seconds following burnout of the first two, then burned out themselves and were jettisoned about one minute later.

With the medium fairing, the Atlas IIAS-Centaur could carry a 19,000-pound payload to low-Earth orbit, an 8,200-pound payload to geosynchronous transfer orbit or a 5,890-pound payload to Earth-escape trajectory.

With the large fairing, the Atlas IIAS-Centaur could carry an 18,500-pound payload to low-Earth orbit, a 7,700-pound payload to geosynchronous transfer orbit or a 5,640-pound payload to Earth-escape trajectory.

TITAN IVB

Classification: Space Launch Vehicle

Length: 177 feet, 2 inches (with IUS upper stage)

Length: 187 feet, 2 inches (maximum with no upper stage)

Length: 207 feet, 2 inches (with Centaur upper stage)

Diameter: 10 feet (first and second stages)

Diameter: 16 feet, 8 inches (payload fairing)

Date of First Cape Canaveral Launch: February 23, 1997

Date of Final Cape Canaveral Launch: April 29, 2005

Number of Cape Canaveral Launches: 13

After 19 Titan IV launches from Cape Canaveral and 7 Titan IV launches from Vandenberg Air Force Base, California, an improved version called the Titan IVB was introduced in early 1997. The Titan IVB increased payload capability by 25 percent over previous Titan IV rockets, which were subsequently renamed Titan IVA.

Although nearly identical to the Titan IVA in other respects, the Titan IVB introduced upgraded solid rocket motors manufactured by Alliant Techsystems, a company which had just recently purchased booster designer Hercules Aerospace Products. Each three-segment solid rocket motor upgrade (SRMU) was 112.4 feet tall by 10.5 feet wide. The solid rocket motors, which burned HTPB solid propellant, could each produce a thrust of 1,700,000 pounds.

First stage thrust of the Titan IVB was improved to 547,100 pounds. Upgraded electronics and guidance, standard vehicle interfaces and new Programmable Aerospace Ground Equipment (PAGE) also enhanced Titan IVB performance over the Titan IVA.

Like the Titan IVA, the Titan IVB could employ a Centaur upper stage, an Inertial Upper Stage (IUS) or no upper stage. With the introduction of the SRMU, specific vehicle payload capacity was improved as follows:

Version 401: Maximum 12,700 pounds
Version 402: Maximum 47,000 pounds
Version 403: Maximum 38,800 pounds
Version 404: Maximum 36,700 pounds
Version 405: Maximum 49,000 pounds

The first Titan IVB was launched from Cape Canaveral Launch Complex 40 on February 23, 1997 and carried a Defense Support Program (DSP) missile detection satellite for the Department of Defense.

This maiden flight of the Titan IVB marked the first time a Cape-launched military Titan mission was declassified. In a change from previous policy, both the nature of the payload and the launch time were made public prior to launch.

ATHENA II

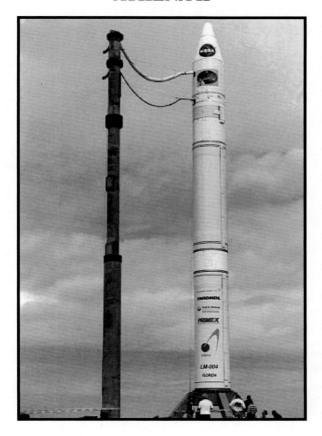

Classification: Space Launch Vehicle

Length: 100 feet

Diameter: 7 feet, 9 inches

Date of First Cape Canaveral Launch: January 6, 1998

Date of Final Cape Canaveral Launch: January 6, 1998

Number of Cape Canaveral Launches: 1

The Lockheed Martin Athena II is a three-stage big brother of the Athena I.

A single Thiokol Castor 120 solid rocket motor provided both first and second stage propulsion for the Athena II, with simply one of the solid rocket motors stacked above the other. Each Castor 120 solid rocket motor was 28 feet, 11 inches long by 7 feet, 9 inches wide.

Each Castor 120 solid rocket motor burned Class 1.3 Hydroxyl-terminated polybutadiene (HTPB) solid propellant and could produce a thrust of 435,000 pounds. The solid rocket motors employed a composite casing, with exhaust nozzle steering provided by blowdown cold gas-powered hydraulic thrust vector control (TVC) actuators.

The Athena II employed an Orbus 21D third stage manufactured by Pratt and Whitney Space Propulsion Operations, Chemical Systems Division. The third stage was 10 feet, 4 inches long by 7 feet, 8 inches wide and, like the Athena II lower stages, burned Class 1.3 HTPB solid fuel.

The third stage could produce 43,723 pounds of thrust. It employed a composite casing, with steering provided by a carbon phenolic nozzle using electromechanical TVC actuators.

Following separation of the third stage, an Orbit Adjust Module (OAM) was ignited. The OAM housed an attitude control system and avionics subsystem, which incorporated guidance and navigation equipment, batteries, telemetry transmitters and command destruct receivers and antennas.

A maximum load of 960 pounds of hydrazine liquid fuel powered the OAM attitude control system, which performed orbital injection corrections, roll control, velocity trim and orbit circularizing maneuvers. The OAM attitude control system was manufactured by Primex Technologies.

Located directly beneath the payload itself, the OAM eventually separated from the payload and performed a contamination and collision avoidance maneuver until its hydrazine fuel is depleted. The maneuver was intended to protect the payload from any potential damage.

The Athena II offered two sizes of payload fairings and three sizes of payload adapters which could be interchanged to accommodate a number of different sized payloads.

Utilizing what its manufacturer called a "stack and shoot" approach to launching payloads, the Athena II could be prepared for launch in just 30 days after its first stage arrived at the launch site.

The rocket was capable of carrying a maximum 4,350-pound payload into low-Earth orbit or a maximum 3,200-pound payload into polar orbit.

It was also capable of sending small payloads into interplanetary trajectory, as was proven by the Athena II launch of the NASA Lunar Prospector on January 6, 1998. The Lunar Prospector weighed 652 pounds and successfully achieved lunar orbit.

DELTA III 8000 SERIES

Classification: Space Launch Vehicle

Length: 128 feet, 2 inches

Diameter (First Stage): 8 feet

Diameter (Upper Stages): 13 feet, 1 inch

Date of First Cape Canaveral Launch: August 26, 1998

Date of Final Cape Canaveral Launch: August 23, 2000

Number of Cape Canaveral Launches: 3

Building directly upon the Delta II 7000 Series of rockets, the Delta III dramatically improved payload capability by introducing larger, more powerful solid rocket boosters and a completely new upper stage configuration.

The Delta III employed the same first stage engine and liquid oxygen tank as the Delta II 7000 series, and shared a number of common technical components which served to trim the development cost of the rocket considerably.

Much about the Delta III, however, was brand new with the introduction of the rocket. This included new Alliant Techsystems solid rocket boosters, sharing the Graphite Epoxy Motors (GEM) name with the solid rocket boosters used in the Delta II 7000 Series. The Delta III was designed to use nine GEM's in all flight applications.

The Delta III GEM's were much larger and more powerful than previous versions. Each GEM measured 65 feet, 8 inches long and had a diameter of 3 feet, 10 inches. Each GEM burned HTPB solid fuel. Six of the

GEM's were ignited at launch, or were "ground-lit". Three of the GEM's were ignited in flight, or were "air-lit".

The ground-lit GEM's could each produce a thrust of about 136,700 pounds while the air-lit GEM's could each produce a thrust of about 141,300 pounds. Three of the ground-lit GEM's employed steerable exhaust nozzles, or thrust vector control, which aided in guiding the Delta III during flight.

Delta III first stage performance was identical to that of the Delta II 7000 Series, but a completely new second stage was employed. A Pratt and Whitney second stage engine, based on the tried and true Pratt and Whitney Centaur upper stage, burned a combination of liquid oxygen and liquid hydrogen and could produce a thrust of about 24,750 pounds.

Previous Delta second stages have burned highly toxic liquid fuels, and the introduction of a second stage that burns liquid oxygen and liquid hydrogen made Delta III launch processing much more safe and cost-effective.

The Delta III was not introduced with a third stage, but could employ a Thiokol solid-fueled third stage similar to that used on Delta II 7000 Series three-stage rockets if necessary.

The standard payload fairing employed on the Delta III had a diameter of 13 feet, 1 inch. In order to support this payload fairing, the Delta III body tapered to a diameter of 13 feet, 1 inch above the first stage liquid oxygen tank.

The Delta III was able to carry a maximum 18,280-pound payload to low-Earth orbit, a maximum 8,400-pound payload to geostationary transfer orbit or a maximum 6,000-pound payload to Earth-escape trajectory.

The performance figure of a maximum 8,400-payload to geostationary transfer orbit, the application required for most commercial communications satellites, represented a remarkable two-fold increase over the performance of the Delta II 7000 series. Despite these improvements, the Delta III suffered two major failures and was retired after just three launches.

ATHENA I

Classification: Space Launch Vehicle

Length: 65 feet

Diameter: 7 feet, 9 inches

Date of First Cape Canaveral Launch: January 26, 1999

Date of Final Cape Canaveral Launch: January 26, 1999

Number of Cape Canaveral Launches: 1

What eventually became known as the Athena rocket program (not to be confused with the Atlantic Research Corporation Athena ballistic missile research program of the mid-1960's) began in January, 1993 as Lockheed decided to capitalize on its rocketry potential.

Lockheed believed that the timing was right to apply its cumulative solid-propellant Polaris, Poseidon and Trident missile technology to the ever-emerging field of launching relatively lightweight payloads into space.

The initial vehicle program that emerged was named Lockheed Launch Vehicle (LLV). After Lockheed merged with Martin Marietta to form Lockheed Martin, the program was renamed Lockheed Martin Launch Vehicle (LMLV).

The core launch vehicle was named LMLV-1, with a larger version named LMLV-2. LMLV-1 was later re-named Athena I, while LMLV-2 was renamed Athena II. A third version, called the Athena III, has also been introduced but to date has not been launched from Cape Canaveral.

The Athena I was a two-stage, solid-fueled rocket capable of carrying a maximum 1,750-pound payload into low-Earth orbit.

A Thiokol Castor 120 solid rocket motor served as the Athena I first stage. The first stage was 28 feet, 9 inches long by 7 feet, 9 inches wide and burned Class 1.3 Hydroxyl-terminated polybutadiene (HTPB) solid propellant. The first stage could produce a thrust of 435,000 pounds at launch.

The first stage motor was housed in a composite case and was steered by blowdown cold gas-powered hydraulic thrust vector control (TVC) actuators. In a typical flight profile, the first stage burned out about 90 seconds after launch, after which the vehicle began an unpowered coast period. The first stage remained attached to the vehicle during this coast to provide aerodynamic stability.

A Pratt and Whitney Orbus 21D solid rocket motor served as the Athena I second stage. The second stage was 10 feet, 4 inches long by 7 feet, 8 inches wide and, like the first stage, burned Class 1.3 HTPB solid propellant. The second stage could produce a thrust of 43,723 pounds.

The second stage motor was housed in a composite case and employed a carbon phenolic nozzle steered by electromechanical TVC actuators. In a typical flight profile, the second stage was fired about 200 seconds after launch and about two seconds following first stage separation. The second stage burned out about 145 seconds after was is fired.

The second stage separated less than one second after it burned out, at which time an Orbit Adjust Module (OAM) attached to the payload was fired. The OAM housed a Primex Technologies attitude control system, as well as an avionics subsystem. The OAM included guidance and navigation controls, batteries, telemetry transmitters, command and destruct receivers and antennas.

The OAM could be ignited, shut down and restarted to perform orbital injection attitude corrections, roll control, velocity trim and orbit circularizing maneuvers. The OAM could carry a maximum 960 pounds of hydrazine liquid fuel. After the OAM completed its role, it separated from the payload and executed a collision avoidance maneuver away from the payload until its fuel was depleted.

The Athena I employed a standard payload fairing which was 14 feet, 1 inch long by 6 feet, 6 inches wide. Considered a "stack and shoot" type of launch vehicle, the Athena I was designed to be launched in as little as 30 days after the first stage arrived at the launch site.

ATLAS IIIA-CENTAUR

Classification: Space Launch Vehicle

Length: 170 feet, 2 inches

Diameter: 10 feet

Date of First Cape Canaveral Launch: May 24, 2000

Date of Final Cape Canaveral Launch: March 13, 2004

Number of Cape Canaveral Launches: 2

In November, 1995 Lockheed-Martin approved plans for a new space launch vehicle called the Atlas IIAR-Centaur. The vehicle design called for some revolutionary innovations for the Atlas program. The one and one-half stage booster/sustainer engine configuration, a trademark of the Atlas for over 40 years, would be replaced by a single stage booster design to make the rocket more efficient and cost-effective.

A follow-up Atlas IIAR-Centaur decision announced by Lockheed-Martin in January, 1996 would confound Atlas missilemen of a bygone era, who sought to validate the Atlas missile as a possible means of laying waste to the former Soviet Union. The company decided that first stage propulsion for the Atlas IIAR-Centaur would be provided by a Russian RD-180 engine, a two-chamber version of the four-chamber RD-170 engine built by NPO Energomash of Russia.

The Atlas IIAR-Centaur was renamed Atlas III-Centaur in April, 1998. Two variants emerged - the Atlas IIIA-Centaur and the Atlas IIIB-Centaur. Of these, the Atlas IIIA-Centaur was the first to be introduced and launched from Cape Canaveral.

As envisioned, first stage propulsion for the Atlas IIIA-Centaur was provided by a Russian RD-180 engine.

The dual-chamber engine was fed by a combination of liquid oxygen and RP-1 (kerosene) liquid fuel. The first stage featured a liquid oxygen tank extended 10 feet longer than that of the Atlas IIAS-Centaur.

The first stage was capable of producing a liftoff thrust of about 860,200 pounds. Switching to a single-stage booster concept for the Atlas IIIA-Centaur resulted in dramatic improvements in production, operation and reliability. Remarkably, the Atlas IIIA-Centaur first stage had about 10,000 fewer parts than the Atlas IIAS-Centaur booster/sustainer engine combination.

Second stage propulsion for the Atlas IIIA-Centaur was provided by a single-engine Centaur, powered by a Pratt and Whitney RL 10A-4-1 engine fed by a combination of liquid oxygen and liquid hydrogen. The second stage was capable of producing a thrust of about 22,300 pounds.

The Atlas IIIA-Centaur could employ either a large or extended large payload fairing. Each payload fairing had a usable diameter of about 12 feet, 6 inches. The Atlas IIIA-Centaur was capable of carrying a maximum 19,004-pound payload to Low Earth-orbit or a maximum 8,950-pound payload to Geostationary Transfer Orbit.

BUMPER-WAC SCALE MODEL

Classification: Model Rocket

Length: 74.8 Inches

Diameter: 7.5 Inches

Weight At Liftoff: 8.5 Pounds

Date of First Cape Canaveral Launch: July 24, 2000

Date of Final Cape Canaveral Launch: July 24, 2000

Number of Cape Canaveral Launches: 1

This 1:8.5 scale model of Bumper #8 was built by Michael Myrick to commemorate the 50th anniversary of the launch of Bumper #8 which occurred on July 24, 1950 and was the first rocket launch from Cape Canaveral. The model rocket was launched not far from Launch Pad 3 on July 24, 2000 as part of an anniversary gathering of about 300 people seated on Launch Pad 3, site of the launch of the real Bumper #8. The launch of the model rocket was carried as an official launch by the 45th Space Wing and in fact the Range Safety Officer gave a final "go" for launch.

The model rocket employed an Aerotech J3505 rocket motor powered by grain in a Dr. Rocket's 38/720 reloadable casing. The motor produced a maximum thrust of 134.5 pounds and an average thrust of 78.7 pounds during a burn time of 1.9 seconds. The rocket reached a maximum altitude of about 1,000 feet. The rocket carried a number of postal covers as ballast, which were later canceled with the official Post Office commemorative Bumper #8 50th anniversary postmark. The flight lasted about three minutes. Unfortunately, the recovery parachutes malfunctioned and the rocket was damaged when it hit the ground.

ATLAS IIIB-CENTAUR

Classification: Space Launch Vehicle

Length: 173 feet

Diameter: 10 feet

Date of First Cape Canaveral Launch: February 21, 2002

Date of Final Cape Canaveral Launch: February 3, 2005

Number of Cape Canaveral Launches: 4

Otherwise identical to the Atlas IIIA, the Atlas IIIB improved performance by employing a two-engine Centaur upper stage, as opposed to a one-engine Centaur upper stage employed on the Atlas IIIA. The two-engine Centaur, featuring two RL-10A engines, could produce a thrust of 41,592 pounds, roughly double the thrust of a single RL-10A engine. In the new configuration, the Atlas IIIB was capable of carrying a 23,630-pound payload to Low-Earth Orbit or a 9,900-pound payload to Geosynchronous Transfer Orbit.

ATLAS V

Classification: Space Launch Vehicle

Length: 191 feet

Diameter: 12 feet, 6 inches

Date of First Cape Canaveral Launch: August 21, 2002

Date of Final Cape Canaveral Launch: Active

Number of Cape Canaveral Launches: Active

Designed as a product of the Air Force Evolved Expendable Launch Vehicle (EELV) program, Atlas V is the latest evolution in the Atlas program. Originally introduced by Lockheed-Martin, the rocket is now operated by United Launch Alliance, a joint venture of Lockheed-Martin and Boeing. Atlas V is a two-stage launch vehicle.

The first stage is comprised of a Russian-built RD-180 engine which burns a combination of liquid oxygen and RP-1 (kerosene) fuel. The first stage can produce a liftoff thrust of 933,406 pounds. The first stage can be augmented by up to five Aerojet strap-on solid rocket boosters. Each booster can produce a thrust of 285,500 pounds.

The Atlas V second stage is comprised of either a one-engine or two-engine RL-10A Centaur upper stage. The Centaur burns a combination of liquid hydrogen and liquid oxygen. The one-engine Centaur can produce a thrust of 22,290 pounds. The two-engine Centaur can produce a thrust of 41,592 pounds.

There are a number of variants of the Atlas V, based upon the size of the payload fairing, the number of solid rocket boosters and the second stage Centaur configuration. Figuring all of the available combinations, the Atlas V can carry a 21,490-pound to 64,860-pound payload to Low-Earth Orbit, or a 10,470-pound to 28,660-pound payload to Geosynchronous Transfer Orbit.

DELTA IV

Classification: Space Launch Vehicle

Length: 235 feet

Diameter: 16.4 feet

Date of First Cape Canaveral Launch: November 20, 2002

Date of Final Cape Canaveral Launch: Active

Number of Cape Canaveral Launches: Active

Designed as a part of the Air Force Evolved Expendable Launch Vehicle (EELV) program, Delta IV is the latest evolution of the long-lived Delta rocket family. The rocket was introduced by Boeing, but is currently operated by United Launch Alliance, a joint venture of Boeing and Lockheed-Martin. Delta IV is a two-stage launch vehicle.

The Delta IV first stage, known as a Common Booster Core, employs a single RS-68 engine, which burns a combination of liquid hydrogen and liquid oxygen. The Common Booster Core can produce a liftoff thrust of 744,737 pounds. In the Delta IV Heavy configuration, three Common Booster Cores are strapped together to increase liftoff thrust approximately three times that of the single Core version.

First stage thrust can be augmented by up to four Graphite Epoxy Motor (GEM) strap-on solid rocket boosters. Each booster can produce a thrust of 185,817 pounds. The Delta IV second stage is powered by a single RL-10B2 engine which burns liquid hydrogen and liquid oxygen and can produce a thrust of 24,740 pounds.

The Delta IV is available in a number of configurations, depending upon fairing size, number of Common Booster Cores and number of solid rocket boosters. Taking into account all of the possible variants, the Delta IV is capable of carrying a 18,900-pound to 56,800-pound payload to Low-Earth Orbit or a 8,500-pound to 23,904-pound payload to Geosynchronous Transfer Orbit.

ARES I-X

Classification: Research Rocket

Length: 327 feet

Diameter: 12 feet, 2 inches

Date of First Cape Canaveral Launch: October 28, 2009

Date of Final Cape Canaveral Launch: October 28, 2009

Number of Cape Canaveral Launches: 1

Ares I-X was a single-stage test vehicle designed to validate flight dynamics of the Ares I, a rocket intended to carry astronauts into space as part of the NASA Constellation program, a follow-up to the Space Shuttle program. The first and only Ares I-X rocket was launched from Kennedy Space Center Launch Pad 39B on October 28, 2009.

The Ares I-X consisted of a powered four-segment solid rocket booster (SRB) as first stage. This stage was directly adapted from the Space Shuttle SRB. The rocket also carried an unpowered fifth segment SRB simulator, an upper stage simulator (USS), simulated Orion Crew Module (CM) and simulated Launch Abort System (LAS). The rocket carried approximately 700 sensors to measure flight dynamics.

During the 2-minute test flight, the vehicle flew to a maximum altitude of 28 miles. The first stage was recovered via parachute about 150 miles downrange of the launch site. NASA reported that all test objectives were met, although the first stage was damaged when it impacted the Atlantic Ocean, due to a recovery parachute malfunction.

215

FALCON 9

Classification: Space Launch Vehicle

Length: 180 feet

Diameter: 12 feet

Date of First Cape Canaveral Launch: June 4, 2010

Date of Final Cape Canaveral Launch: Active

Number of Cape Canaveral Launches: Active

Falcon 9 is a two-stage, liquid oxygen and RP-1 (kerosene) powered rocket manufactured by Space Exploration Technologies Corporation (SpaceX).

The Falcon 9 first stage is powered by nine Merlin engines, each capable of producing an initial thrust of 125,000 pounds. This combination provided a total liftoff thrust of about 1.1 million pounds.

The Falcon 9 second stage is powered by a single Merlin engine, capable of producing an initial thrust of 125,000 pounds. The Falcon 9 as introduced was capable of carrying a 23,050-pound payload to Low-Earth Orbit, or a 10,000-pound payload to Geosynchronous Transfer Orbit.

Of particular importance to NASA is the SpaceX-designed and built Dragon space capsule, which is intended to carry supplies and astronauts to the International Space Station.

FALCON 9 VERSION 1.1

Length: 224.4 feet

Diameter: 12 feet

In 2013, SpaceX introduced an improved version of the Falcon 9 designated Falcon 9 Version 1.1 which vastly improved performance over the Falcon 9 as initially introduced. Among other improvements, Falcon 9 Version 1.1 featured improved Merlin engines, stretched fuel tanks and the ability to carry either a Dragon capsule or composite payload fairing.

The Falcon 9 Version 1.1 first stage burns liquid oxygen and RP-1 liquid fuel and is comprised of nine Merlin engines. Total thrust at liftoff is approximately 1.323 million pounds. The first stage burns for about 180 seconds after launch. The entire first stage array is designed to be recovered on a barge at sea or on land, refurbished and re-flown. The Falcon 9 Version 1.1 second stage is comprised of a single Merlin engine capable of producing a thrust of 180,000 pounds. The second stage burns for about 375 seconds after ignition and can be restarted multiple times as needed.

The rocket can carry either a Dragon capsule or composite payload fairing. The pressurized Dragon capsule measures 23.6 feet high by 12 feet wide and is designed to carry cargo and astronauts to the International Space Station. The composite payload fairing measures 43 feet high by 17.1 feet wide. The rocket can carry a maximum 28,991-pound payload to Low-Earth Orbit or a maximum 10,692-pound payload to Geosynchronous Transfer Orbit.

FALCON 9 FULL THRUST VERSION

Length: 229.6 feet

Diameter: 12 feet

The Falcon 9 Full Thrust Version is currently in use. The vehicle employs liquid oxygen that is super cold, nearly at its freezing point. The use of this denser fuel coupled with an extended fuel tank allows more fuel to be loaded into the rocket, increasing liftoff thrust and burn time. First stage thrust is increased to 1.71 million pounds at liftoff. Second stage thrust is 210,000 pounds.

The vehicle is capable of carrying a 50,265-pound payload to Low-Earth Orbit, an 18,300-pound payload to Geosynchronous Transfer Orbit or an 8,860-pound payload on a Mars trajectory. The Falcon 9 program to date has achieved several milestones, including landing a first stage booster on a barge at sea and on land, as well as successfully re-flying a flown orbital class booster.

CREW DRAGON

Classification: Space Capsule

Height: 23.6 feet

Diameter: 12 feet

Date of First Cape Canaveral Launch: May 6, 2015

Date of Final Cape Canaveral Launch: May 6, 2015

Number of Cape Canaveral Launches: 1

Crew Dragon is a manned space capsule introduced by SpaceX for the purpose of ferrying astronauts to and from the International Space Station. A Crew Dragon space capsule was launched from Launch Pad 40 on May 6, 2015 to validate that the spacecraft can fire away from a rocket in the case of an in-flight emergency. While the Crew Dragon will ultimately be launched atop a Falcon 9 rocket, the Crew Dragon for this test flight was launched from the ground. The Crew Dragon is powered by eight Super Draco engines which burn hydrazine/nitrogen tetroxide liquid fuel and can each produce a thrust of 15,000 pounds.

The Super Draco engines are integrated directly into the sides of the spacecraft, as opposed to being located atop the spacecraft as in other escape rocket applications. This configuration allows astronauts escape capability from the launch pad all the way to orbit. It also allows the Super Draco engines to fire as retrorockets when the spacecraft is recovered on land.

In the test flight, the eight Super Draco engines were ground lit simultaneously and reached maximum thrust in a matter of seconds, propelling the spacecraft off the launch pad. After a half second of vertical flight, the spacecraft pitched toward the ocean. The Crew Dragon traveled from 0 to 100 m.p.h. in 1.2 seconds, eventually reaching a maximum velocity of 345 m.p.h. The abort burn was terminated once all fuel was consumed, then the spacecraft coasted to its highest point.

The trunk of the spacecraft was then jettisoned and Crew Dragon began a slow rotation with its heat shield reoriented toward the ground. Small drogue parachutes were deployed following trunk separation. Once the drogue parachutes stabilized the spacecraft, three main parachutes were deployed to further slow the spacecraft before splashdown. Less than two minutes after ignition, Crew Dragon splashed down just downrange of the launch pad. While this test was unmanned, Crew Dragon carried a dummy equipped with a number of sensors. Sensors indicated that had astronauts been aboard, they would have been fine.

Cape Canaveral Launch Vehicles Quick Look Facts

From July 1950 to May 2017

Vehicle	First Launch Date	Final Launch Date	Number of Launches	Customer	Vehicle Type
Bumper-WAC	07/24/50	07/29/50	2	Army	Research Rocket
Lark	10/25/50	07/08/53	40	Air Force	Winged Missile
Matador	06/20/51	06/01/61	286	Air Force	Winged Missile
Snark	08/29/52	12/05/60	97	Air Force	Winged Missile
Bomarc A	09/10/52	04/21/59	63	Air Force	Winged Missile
RV-A-10	02/11/53	03/25/53	4	Army	Research Rocket
Redstone	08/20/53	06/26/61	27	Army	Ballistic Missile
X-17	05/23/55	03/21/57	37	Air Force	Research Rocket
Navaho X-10	08/19/55	01/26/59	15	Air Force	Winged Missile
Jupiter A	03/14/56	01/14/58	20	Army	Ballistic Missile
Jupiter C	09/20/56	08/08/57	3	Army	Research Rocket
Navaho XSM-64	11/06/56	11/18/58	11	Air Force	Winged Missile
Vanguard	12/08/56	09/18/59	14	Navy/NASA	Space Launch Vehicle
Thor	01/25/57	07/18/62	51	Air Force	Ballistic Missile
Jupiter	03/01/57	01/22/63	36	Army	Ballistic Missile
Bull Goose	03/13/57	12/05/58	20	Air Force	Winged Missile
Polaris FTV	04/13/57	06/24/58	18	Navy	Research Rocket
Atlas A	06/11/57	06/03/58	8	Air Force	Ballistic Missile
Juno I	01/31/58	10/22/58	6	Army	Space Launch Vehicle
Thor-Able O	04/23/58	07/23/58	3	Air Force	Research Rocket
Bold Orion	05/26/58	10/13/59	12	Air Force	Ballistic Missile
Atlas B	07/19/58	02/04/59	9	Air Force	Ballistic Missile
Jason	08/14/58	09/02/58	6	Air Force	Research Rocket
Thor-Able I	08/17/58	11/08/58	3	Air Force/NASA	Space Launch Vehicle
ALBM-199C	09/05/58	06/04/59	3	Air Force	Ballistic Missile
Polaris A1	09/24/58	09/04/63	109	Navy	Ballistic Missile
Juno II	12/06/58	05/24/61	10	Army/NASA	Space Launch Vehicle
Atlas-Score	12/18/58	12/18/58	1	NASA	Space Launch Vehicle
Atlas C	12/23/58	08/24/59	6	Air Force	Ballistic Missile
Thor-Able II	01/23/59	04/01/60	8	Air Force/NASA	Research Rocket/SLV
Titan I	02/06/59	01/29/62	47	Air Force	Ballistic Missile
Alpha Draco	02/16/59	04/27/59	3	Air Force	Research Rocket
Atlas D	04/14/59	01/23/61	33	Air Force	Ballistic Missile
Hound Dog	04/23/59	08/30/65	77	Air Force	Winged Missile
Bomarc B	05/27/59	04/15/60	7	Air Force	Winged Missile
Thor-Able III	08/07/59	08/07/59	1	NASA	Space Launch Vehicle
Mace	10/29/59	07/17/63	44	Air Force	Winged Missile
Atlas-Able	11/26/59	12/15/60	3	NASA	Space Launch Vehicle
Pershing I	02/25/60	04/24/63	56	Army	Ballistic Missile
Atlas-Agena A	02/26/60	05/24/60	2	Air Force	Space Launch Vehicle
Thor-Able IV	03/11/60	03/11/60	1	NASA	Space Launch Vehicle
Thor-Able Star	04/13/60	10/31/62	11	Air Force	Space Launch Vehicle
Delta	05/13/60	09/18/62	12	NASA	Space Launch Vehicle
Mercury-Atlas	07/29/60	05/15/63	9	NASA	Space Launch Vehicle
Blue Scout Junior	09/21/60	06/09/65	10	Air Force	Research Rocket
Atlas E	10/11/60	02/25/64	19	Air Force	Ballistic Missile
Polaris A2	11/10/60	09/02/71	222	Navy	Ballistic Missile
Mercury-Redstone	11/21/60	07/21/61	6	NASA	Space Launch Vehicle
Blue Scout I	01/07/61	04/12/62	3	Air Force	Space Launch Vehicle
Minuteman I	02/01/61	09/29/64	54	Air Force	Ballistic Missile
Blue Scout II	03/03/61	04/12/61	2	Air Force	Research Rocket
Atlas F	08/08/61	04/01/64	14	Air Force	Ballistic Missile
Atlas-Agena B	08/23/61	06/06/66	12	NASA	Space Launch Vehicle
Saturn I Block I	10/27/61	03/28/63	4	NASA	Research Rocket
Mercury-Scout	11/01/61	11/01/61	1	NASA	Space Launch Vehicle
Titan II	03/16/62	04/09/64	23	Air Force	Ballistic Missile

Vehicle	First Launch Date	Final Launch Date	Number of Launches	Customer	Vehicle Type
Skybolt	04/19/62 – 12/22/62		6	Air Force	Ballistic Missile
Atlas-Centaur (1962)	05/08/62 – 08/11/65		6	NASA	Space Launch Vehicle
Polaris A3	08/07/62 – 02/20/79		194	Navy	Ballistic Missile
Delta A	10/02/62 – 10/27/62		2	NASA	Space Launch Vehicle
Delta B	12/13/62 – 03/19/64		10	NASA	Space Launch Vehicle
Thor-Asset	09/18/63 – 02/23/65		6	Air Force	Research Rocket
Atlas-Agena D	10/16/63 – 04/06/78		35	Air Force/NASA	Space Launch Vehicle
Saturn I Block II	01/29/64 – 07/30/65		6	NASA	Space Launch Vehicle
Gemini-Titan II	04/08/64 – 11/11/66		12	NASA	Space Launch Vehicle
Atlas-Antares	04/14/64 – 05/22/65		2	NASA	Research Rocket
Delta D	08/19/64 – 04/06/65		2	NASA	Space Launch Vehicle
Titan III-A	09/01/64 – 05/06/65		4	Air Force	Space Launch Vehicle
Minuteman II	09/24/64 – 03/14/70		21	Air Force	Ballistic Missile
Delta C	10/03/64 – 01/22/69		12	NASA	Space Launch Vehicle
Titan III-C	06/18/65 – 03/06/82		36	Air Force/NASA	Space Launch Vehicle
Delta E	11/06/65 – 12/05/68		13	NASA	Space Launch Vehicle
Saturn IB	02/26/66 – 07/15/75		9	NASA	Space Launch Vehicle
Atlas-Centaur (1966)	04/07/66 – 07/25/90		63	Air Force/NASA	Space Launch Vehicle
Delta G	12/14/66 – 09/07/67		2	NASA	Space Launch Vehicle
Saturn V Apollo	11/09/67 – 12/07/72		12	NASA	Space Launch Vehicle
Minuteman III	08/16/68 – 12/14/70		17	Air Force	Ballistic Missile
Poseidon	08/16/68 – 04/30/90		268	Navy	Ballistic Missile
Delta M	09/18/68 – 02/02/71		12	NASA	Space Launch Vehicle
Delta N	02/26/69 – 09/29/71		4	NASA	Space Launch Vehicle
Delta L	08/27/69 – 08/27/69		1	NASA	Space Launch Vehicle
Delta M6	03/13/71 – 03/13/71		1	NASA	Space Launch Vehicle
Delta 1000 Series	09/22/72 – 06/21/75		6	NASA	Space Launch Vehicle
Pershing IA	02/21/73 – 10/13/83		100	Army	Ballistic Missile
Saturn V Skylab	05/14/73 – 05/14/73		1	NASA	Space Launch Vehicle
Delta 2000 Series	01/18/74 – 08/09/79		34	NASA	Space Launch Vehicle
Titan III-E Centaur	02/11/74 – 09/05/77		7	NASA	Space Launch Vehicle
SRAM	08/20/74 – 07/26/83		31	Air Force	Cruise Missile
Delta 3000 Series	12/12/75 – 03/24/89		33	Air Force/NASA	Space Launch Vehicle
Trident I	01/18/77 – 12/18/01		162	Navy/Royal Navy	Ballistic Missile
Chevaline	09/12/77 – 05/10/87		34	Navy/Royal Navy	Ballistic Missile
Space Shuttle Columbia	04/12/81 – 01/16/03		28	NASA	Space Launch Vehicle
Penguin	02/18/82 – 04/08/82		9	Navy	Cruise Missile
Pershing II	07/22/82 – 03/21/88		49	Army	Ballistic Missile
Titan 34D	10/30/82 – 09/04/89		8	Air Force	Space Launch Vehicle
Space Shuttle Challenger	04/04/83 – 01/28/86		10	NASA	Space Launch Vehicle
Space Shuttle Discovery	08/30/84 – 02/24/11		39	NASA	Space Launch Vehicle
Space Shuttle Atlantis	10/03/85 – 07/08/11		33	NASA	Space Launch Vehicle
Trident II	01/15/87 – Active		160	Navy/Royal Navy	Ballistic Missile
Loft 1	11/17/88 – 11/17/88		1	Commercial	Research Rocket
Delta II 6000 Series	02/14/89 – 07/24/92		16	Commercial/Air Force/NASA	Space Launch Vehicle
Titan IVA	06/14/89 – 08/12/98		14	Air Force	Space Launch Vehicle
Delta 4000 Series	08/27/89 – 06/12/90		2	Commercial	Space Launch Vehicle
Commercial Titan III	12/31/89 – 09/25/92		4	Commercial/NASA	Space Launch Vehicle
Delta II 7000 Series	11/26/90 – 09/10/11		94	Commercial/Air Force/NASA	Space Launch Vehicle
Starbird	12/18/90 – 05/28/93		3	Air Force	Research Rocket
Atlas I-Centaur	04/18/91 – 04/25/97		10	Commercial/Air Force/NASA	Space Launch Vehicle
Prospector	06/18/91 – 06/18/91		1	NASA	Research Rocket
Aries I	08/20/91 – 10/14/91		2	Air Force	Research Rocket
Atlas II-Centaur	12/07/91 – 07/25/96		9	Commercial/Air Force	Space Launch Vehicle
Space Shuttle Endeavour	05/07/92 – 05/16/11		25	NASA	Space Launch Vehicle
Atlas IIA-Centaur	06/10/92 – 12/04/02		24	Commercial/Air Force/NASA	Space Launch Vehicle
Pegasus XL	02/09/93 – Active		6	Commercial/NASA	Space Launch Vehicle
Atlas IIAS-Centaur	12/15/93 – 08/31/04		27	Commercial/NASA/Air Force	Space Launch Vehicle
Titan IVB	02/23/97 – 04/29/05		13	Air Force/NASA	Space Launch Vehicle

Vehicle	First Launch Date	Final Launch Date	Number of Launches	Customer	Vehicle Type
Athena II	01/06/98	01/06/98	1	NASA	Space Launch Vehicle
Delta III 8000 Series	08/26/98	08/23/00	3	Commercial	Space Launch Vehicle
Athena I	01/26/99	01/26/99	1	Commercial	Space Launch Vehicle
Atlas IIIA-Centaur	05/24/00	03/13/04	2	Commercial	Space Launch Vehicle
Bumper Scale Model	07/24/00	07/24/00	1	Air Force	Model Rocket
Atlas IIIB-Centaur	02/21/02	02/03/05	4	Air Force, NASA	Space Launch Vehicle
Atlas V	08/21/02	Active	58	Air Force/NASA/Commercial	Space Launch Vehicle
Delta IV	11/20/02	Active	29	Air Force, NASA	Space Launch Vehicle
Ares I-X	10/28/09	10/28/09	1	NASA	Space Launch Vehicle
Falcon 9	06/04/10	Active	31	Commercial/NASA/Air Force	Space Launch Vehicle
Crew Dragon	05/06/15	05/06/15	1	Commercial	Space Capsule

About the Author

Cliff Lethbridge has been a freelance radio and print journalist covering Cape Canaveral and the Kennedy Space Center since 1979. He has submitted stories to over 50 news organizations. His credits include CBS Radio News, CNN Radio News, USA Radio News, Salem Radio News, Florida Network Radio News, Space. com and Reuters. He is one of only a few journalists who covered the Space Shuttle program from its beginning in 1981 to its end in 2011.

In 1996, Lethbridge founded Spaceline, Inc. which is dedicated to covering the past, present and future of Cape Canaveral through its website, www.spaceline.org which features dozens of articles related to the Cape and the U.S. space program with an emphasis on history. In 2017, he created a sister website at www.shop-spaceline.com dedicated to offering a diverse selection of space collectibles for sale, including items flown in space and astronaut autographs.

Lethbridge has written two previous books. His first was entitled "The Story of Explorer I – America's First Satellite" released in 1998 to commemorate the 40th anniversary of its historic launch. His second book, entitled "Cape Canaveral – 500 Years of History – 50 Years of Rocketry" was released in 2000 to commemorate the 50th anniversary of the first rocket launch from the Cape. In addition to his reporting activities, Lethbridge is the Senior Announcer at WCIF-FM in Melbourne, Florida.

Cape Canaveral "Missile Row" looking south, 1963

66729130R10129

Made in the USA
Lexington, KY
22 August 2017